More Than Counting

Whole Math Activities for Preschool and Kindergarten

by
Sally Moomaw
and
Brenda Hieronymus

Redleaf Press

Published by: Redleaf Press
                  a division of Resources for Child Caring
                  450 N. Syndicate, Suite 5
                  St. Paul, MN 55104

Distributed by: Gryphon House
                  Mailing Address:
                  P.O. Box 207
                  Beltsville, MD 20704-0207

ISBN: 1-884834-03-5

Moomaw, Sally, 1948-
        More than counting : whole math activities for preschool
and kindergarten / by Sally Moomaw and Brenda Hieronymus.
                  p.   cm.
        Includes bibliographical references.
        ISBN 1-884834-03-5 (alk. paper)
        1. Mathematics—Study and teaching (Preschool)
        2. Mathematics—Study and teaching—Activity programs.
        I. Hieronymus, Brenda, 1945 -   . II. Title
        QA135.5.M6153   1995
        372.7'044—dc20
                                              95-13460   CIP

To Anne Dorsey

and to the children, parents, and teachers of the
Arlitt Child Development Center, University of Cincinnati

Acknowledgements

We wish to thank Anne Dorsey for sharing her extensive knowledge and special insights about children and mathematics, for reading and commenting on the manuscript, and for her leadership, encouragement, and inspiration that have led to both the development of the mathematics curriculum and the writing of this book.

We are greatly indebted to Charles J. Moomaw for his extensive work in preparing the manuscript. We thank David C. Baxter of PhotoGraphic Services, University of Cincinnati, for photographing the games and materials; William L. Heckle for his photographs of the children playing gross-motor math games; Mary Ann McPherson and Ellen Lynch for reading the manuscript and offering comments; Elizabeth Van Fleet and Deborah Ravenscraft for helping make the games; and the University of Cincinnati Arlitt Child and Family Research and Education Center for the use of its facilities for the photography.

We thank Kidstamps, Incorporated, P.O. Box 18699, Cleveland Heights, Ohio 44118, for permission to photograph imprints from their stamps used with the games.

All stickers used in the activities described and photographed in this book are manufactured by Mrs. Grossman's Paper Company, 77 Digital Drive, Novato, California 94949, ©MGPC. We appreciate their permission to photograph the materials.

We especially thank the children who allowed us to photograph them while they played the math games: Andy, Bené, Claire, Drew, John, Kimmy, Lee Ann, Maria, Nancy, Stephen, and Whitney.

Contents

Preface

How to Use This Book ix

Chapter 1   Introduction to Whole Math

The Whole-Math Classroom 2

The Whole-Math Child 4

The Whole-Math Teacher 6

Chapter 2   Math Manipulatives

Teachers' Questions 11

Math Manipulative Activities

  2.1 Strawberry Picking Game 22

  2.2 Bird Nests and Eggs 23

  2.3 Heart Game .24

  2.4 Marble Game 25

  2.5 Nature Game 26

  2.6 Pom-Pom Game 27

  2.7 Bean Game .28

  2.8 People Game 29

  2.9 Palm Tree Pegboard Game 30

  2.10 Doghouse Game 31

  2.11 Shape Sorter Game 32

  2.12 Clothespin Game 33

  2.13 Marble Can Addends Game 34

  2.14 "Three Little Bats" Interactive Song Chart. .35

  2.15 "10 in the Bed" Interactive Song Chart . .36

  2.16 Trick or Treat Interactive Chart 37

  2.17 "5 Little Monkeys" Finger Puppets 38

  2.18 "5 Little Monkeys" Manipulative Game. .39

  2.19 "10 in the Bed" Manipulative Game 40

  2.20 Caterpillar Manipulative Game 42

  2.21 "Five Little Ducks" Manipulative Game. .44

  2.22 Animal Flannelboard 45

  2.23 Pretzel Magnetic Board 46

  2.24 "Five Little Ducks" Counting Book 47

2.25 "Salty Pretzel" Counting Book 48
2.26 Cookie Sharing Manipulative Game 50
2.27 Recycling Collection Game 51
Interactions with Manipulatives 52

Chapter 3 Collections
Teachers' Questions 55
Collection Activities
3.1 Keys 62
3.2 Buttons 63
3.3 Shoes 64
3.4 Hats 66
3.5 Paper Clips 67
3.6 Clothespins & Note Clips 68
3.7 Bottle Caps & Lids 70
3.8 Sea Shells 71
3.9 Bells 72
3.10 International Money 73
3.11 Jewels 74
3.12 Bandages 76
3.13 Pom-Poms 78
3.14 Rings 79
3.15 Nuts 80
3.16 Snowflakes 82
Interactions with Collections 84

Chapter 4 Grid Games
Teachers' Questions 85
Grid Game Activities
4.1 Silhouette Grid 94
4.2 Pinwheel Grid .95
4.3 Rabbit Grid 96
4.4 Vegetable Grid 97
4.5 Squirrel Grid 98
4.6 Leaf Grid 1 99
4.7 Teddy Bear Grid 100
4.8 Snowman Grid 102
4.9 Toothbrush Grid 103
4.10 Letter Grid .104
4.11 Snowflake Grid 1 105
4.12 Jewels for a Crown 106
4.13 Leaf Grid 2 .107
4.14 Palm Tree Grid 108
4.15 Chicken Grid 109
4.16 Snowflake Grid 2 110

4.17 Baby Grid 111
4.18 Balloons 112
4.19 Dot Grid 114
Interactions with Grid Games 115

Chapter 5 Path Games

Teachers' Questions 117
Path Game Activities
5.1 Doctor Short Path Game 126
5.2 Jewel Short Path Game 127
5.3 Teddy Bear Short Path Game 128
5.4 Balloon Short Path Game 130
5.5 Chicken Short Path Game 132
5.6 Letter Short Path Game 134
5.7 Autumn Short Path Game 136
5.8 Planting Short Path Game 137
5.9 Treasure Chest Short Path Game 138
5.10 Winter Short Path Game 140
5.11 Apple Short Path Game 142
5.12 Autumn Continuous Path
     Collection Game 144
5.13 Bandage Long Path Game 146
5.14 Teddy Bear Long Path Game 148
5.15 Farm Long Path Game 150
5.16 Letter Long Path Game 152
5.17 Castle Long Path Game 154
5.18 Autumn Long Path Game 156
5.19 Planting Long Path Game 158
5.20 Treasure Chest Long Path Game 160
5.21 Winter Long Path Game 162
5.22 Apple Long Path Game 164
5.23 Balloon Long Path Game 166
Interactions with Path Games 168

Chapter 6 Graphing

Teachers' Questions 169
Graphing Activities
6.1 Hair Color Graph 176
6.2 Favorite Ice Cream Graph 177
6.3 Shoe Fastener Graph 178
6.4 Author Unit Graph 180
6.5 Apple Tasting Graph 182
6.6 Pumpkin Growing Prediction Chart 184
6.7 Chicken Pox Graph 186
6.8 Favorite Character Graph 188

      6.9 Recording Permission Slips 190
      6.10 Individual Graph 191
    Interactions with Graphs 192

Chapter 7 Math and Gross-Motor Play

    Teachers' Questions 195
    Gross-Motor Math Activities
      7.1 Copy Cat Number Song 200
      7.2 Ball Counting Song 201
      7.3 People Mover Path Game 202
      7.4 Forward and Back 203
      7.5 Bear Hunt Game 204
      7.6 Ramp Bowling 206
      7.7 Stack and Fall 208
      7.8 Straw-Blowing Cotton Swabs 209
      7.9 Target Ball 210
      7.10 Ski-Ball 211
      7.11 Pendulum Bottle Game 212
      7.12 Pulley Transfer Game 214
      7.13 Animal Mail-Order Game 215
    Interactions with Gross-Motor Play 216

Chapter 8 The Math Suitcase

    Teachers' Questions 219
    Math Suitcase Activities
      8.1 Cloud Math Suitcase 224
      8.2 Flower Basket Math Suitcase 225
      8.3 Snowman Math Suitcase 226
      8.4 Dinosaur Math Suitcase 227
      8.5 Butterfly Math Suitcase 228
      8.6 "Party On" Math Suitcase 229
    Interactions with the Math Suitcase 230

Appendix

    Sample Assessment Forms
      A.1 Class Assessment Form 234
      A.2 Individual Assessment Form 235
      A.3 Class Assessment Form for Collections . .236
      A.4 Individual Assessment Form
         for Collections 237
    Songs
      B.1 Three Little Bats 238
      B.2 Salty Pretzels 238
      B.3 It Was Snow 239

Glossary .242

Preface

More Than Counting is an extensive sampling of a "whole-math" curriculum that has been evolving since the publication of constructivist math texts over the past decade, particularly Constance Kamii's *Number in Preschool and Kindergarten* (NAEYC, 1982). Developed by teachers at the Arlitt Child Development Center of the University of Cincinnati and tested for over ten years in preschool and kindergarten classrooms, this whole-math curriculum is the result of years of collaboration, study, and modification.

Our exploration of new curriculum possibilities began with a recognition that traditional materials, including most of the commercial math manipulatives, did not effectively advance children's mathematical thinking. As we began to try some of the ideas of researchers such as Kamii, a new direction began to emerge. Teachers modified materials, designed games, piloted them in the classrooms, and discussed the results. After lengthy experimentation, it became apparent that certain design features and types of games were superior in promoting the Arlitt Center's goals of facilitating children's construction of mathematical knowledge. The games and materials in this book are descendants of those models.

Many of the materials in this book are games. All of them are fun. They are designed to appeal to the interests of girls as well as boys, thereby encouraging all children to explore the mathematical possibilities inherent in them. It is important for teachers to realize that these activities are not additions to enrich the curriculum; they *are* the curriculum. It is through their interactions with these materials and with one another that children construct mathematical concepts.

The activities in this book were designed for preschool and kindergarten children, age three and older. Some of the materials contain small pieces. If teachers of younger children wish to adapt some of these activities, they should be certain to use pieces that young children cannot swallow. The descriptions and photographs of the materials are included only for the purpose of information; none of the materials are for sale.

We recognize that some teachers may not feel comfortable about their own math abilities. We feel, however, that it is vital for us as teachers to demonstrate our own excitement and confidence in solving everyday math problems. We hope the activities included in this book will ease teacher anxiety about developing math curriculum. Teachers can copy and implement the ideas or use them as models in designing their own activities.

In the interest of equality, we have dealt with gender pronouns by alternating between masculine and feminine forms throughout the book, both when discussing children and teachers.

The children we teach vary in age. Some are barely three, while others have already turned six. They come from many different cultures, countries, and family backgrounds. They speak many different languages. They are socioeconomically diverse. Some have disabilities. Yet they all enjoy math. All are active thinkers and problem solvers. All experience enormous growth in mathematical concepts during the school year. Most of all, all emerge confident in their mathematical abilities.

How to Use This Book

More Than Counting is designed to assist early childhood educators in providing a mathematics curriculum rooted in thinking and problem solving. It is intended for new as well as experienced teachers. No prerequisite knowledge is assumed; therefore we define and discuss the basic math concepts that emerge in young children. We also provide a glossary of the mathematical and educational concepts that appear in this book.

An introductory chapter is followed by seven curriculum chapters that discuss math manipulatives, collections, grid games, path games, graphing, math and gross-motor play, and the "math suitcase." The activities presented in this book are adaptable to multiple levels of preschool and kindergarten children.

Each chapter is divided into three sections. The first section, "Teachers' Questions," provides background information and suggestions for teachers on each of the chapter topics. For ease of use, we selected a question/answer format that features the questions we most frequently encounter. These are the types of questions professionals ask us in courses or workshops, parents ask us from time to time, or we ask each other or other teachers as we collaborate to design new materials. The second, and by far the lengthiest, section of each chapter, is composed of activities that illustrate how to make the materials and provide suggestions for implementation. Each chapter ends with several anecdotes that describe real-life interactions with some of the materials. Although the anecdotes are real, the names have been changed to respect confidentiality. We hope the anecdotes convey some of the excitement and enthusiasm of a whole-math classroom. To assist teachers in assessing their children's progress, we have included assessment forms in the appendix, section A. Section B of the appendix contains three songs that are cited on the activity pages.

Over 100 activities are included in this book. Each one has been field tested and modified accordingly. The activity pages in this book contain the following information:

▲ A photograph of the material appears on each activity page so teachers can clearly visualize the math activity.

▲ **Materials**—Each activity page contains a detailed description of the materials that are required to reproduce the activity. Additional material-related headings that may appear on activity pages are the following:

    ▲ **Book** or **Song**—Where appropriate, we identify the book or song upon which the activity is based. If the book or song is **predictable,** we indicate this in the heading.

    ▲ **Description**—Each graphing and gross-motor activity (chapters 6 and 7) contains a detailed description of how the materials are used.

    ▲ **Directions**—A few activities (2.24, 2.25, 8.5, and 8.6) include directions that would not otherwise be obvious.

    ▲ **Possible Attributes**—Collection activities (chapter 3) identify the attributes that children may associate with the particular collection.

    ▲ **Starter Set**—Collection activities also suggest the number of pieces to include in the starter set.

▲ **Child's Level**—Since all of the activities are self-leveling, children at various stages of development will use them in different ways. Thus, there is no one correct way to play any game in this book. However, each activity was designed to be especially suitable for children at a specific level of mathematical thinking. Under this heading we identify the level of development that the material primarily targets.

▲ **What to Look For**—A number of scenarios are described to guide teachers as they watch a range of children interact with the materials. The descriptions are typical but are not meant to be inclusive. Teachers may observe that children respond to the materials in numerous other ways. (This heading and the headings that follow, all of which refer to classroom situations, do not appear in chapter 8, which describes take-home materials.)

▲ **Modifications**—We list ways in which to vary the activities. The teacher may find it necessary to increase or decrease the difficulty of the material to accommodate the mathematical level of individual children. Other modifications simply provide variety. For collection activities (chapter 3), this heading appears as **What to Add**. Modifications are not suggested for activities in chapter 6 since most of the graphs will naturally change each time the children vote.

▲ **Questions to Extend Thinking**—A large part of the teacher's role in a constructivist classroom is to observe children's interactions with materials and then ask leading questions that encourage the development of higher levels of thinking. We provide teachers with ideas of possible questions to ask for each activity.

▲ **Integrated Curriculum Activities**—Many teachers design their curriculum around a central theme or a particular book. This motivates children interested in a thematic topic to explore it throughout the curriculum. We suggest ways to coordinate the math material with other math activities and with other areas of the curriculum.

▲ **Helpful Hints**—Check our suggestions for each activity. They may help you to avoid our bungles.

Introduction to Whole Math

- ▲ Claire rolls a ball at a target made of one-liter bottles and knocks over three.

- ▲ Jeffrey and Amanda disagree about how to distribute mats for group time.

- ▲ Peter scoops pebbles and tiny dinosaurs out of the sensory table and places one pebble by each dinosaur.

- ▲ Momoko and Rosetta consult a waiting list to figure out how many people are ahead of them.

- ▲ Anne, Nader, and David take turns rolling two dice, counting the dots, and moving their wooden snow-men along a path.

What do all of these events have in common? Each involves mathematical thinking, and all are an integrated part of the curriculum.

In the traditional approach to teaching mathematics, teachers attempt to instruct children about mathematical concepts. Children are told how and when to count, how to add and subtract, and how to solve problems as a separate curricular activity. Often the solutions, to say nothing of the problems, have no meaning to the children.

If teachers instead take advantage of the everyday situations in which mathematics arises, they can create an environment where children continually *construct* math concepts. If teachers create an interactive curriculum where children can collaborate on solving real math problems that arise out of their use of the materials, children will think even more about mathematical relationships. If teachers value children's abilities to generate unique solutions to problems, then children come to believe in *themselves* as the problem solvers. Math becomes exciting. Math permeates the day. We call this **whole math.**

The Whole-Math Classroom

What is whole math?

Whole math is an approach to mathematics education that stimulates children to create mathematical relationships out of real-life situations. It is analogous to the whole-language approach to teaching reading and writing.[1] Just as research in whole language recognizes that children construct the concepts of written language by interacting with print in their environment, so whole-math educators acknowledge that children learn mathematical concepts best by attempting to solve real math problems.[2]

In whole-math classrooms, children are surrounded by events with math-rich potential: dividing playdough materials, figuring out who collected more acorns, classifying materials before returning them to their appropriate places, adding a basketball score. As children devise strategies to solve the myriad problems they confront each day, they construct the very mathematical concepts that teachers for decades have tried with limited success to directly teach.

What constitutes a math-rich classroom environment?

In a math-rich environment, math possibilities permeate the entire classroom. As children play and create, mathematical concepts emerge naturally. The following examples depict the type of mathematical situations that may arise in various areas of the classroom.

ONE-TO-ONE CORRESPONDENCE
▲ In the dramatic-play area, several children sit in the "pizza parlor" while one acts as the server. The server brings one plate, one cup, and one piece of fruit for each "customer."

▲ In the art area, Peggy glues one cotton ball onto each square of a piece of one-inch graph paper.

▲ At group time, the children imitate the teacher as he claps the children's names with one clap per syllable.

Zak	Ab- by	Ma- ry Ann	Hes- sam	Con- nie
clap	clap clap	clap clap clap	clap clap	clap clap

SORTING AND CLASSIFICATION
▲ In the science area, Kai-Jye sorts through a basket of acorns and groups them by size. After he leaves, another child regroups the acorns according to whether or not they have a cap.

▲ In the block area, the children begin to return blocks to shelves that are labeled with pictures corresponding to the shapes of the blocks. Emily stops and tells the others that the teacher "did it wrong," meaning that she disagrees with the labeling of the shelves. Emily proposes that the cylinder blocks should be grouped with the column blocks because "they all stand up tall." The teacher had provided separate shelf units for the cylinders and the columns.

▲ In the dramatic-play area, children begin to put away materials. Larry searches for all the plastic fruit, while Maggie collects the silverware. Ching-Wei hangs up all the vests. (The design of the area can encourage classification of materials. If the teacher provides only a large box for storage, the children are likely to merely throw all materials into the box rather than classify them beforehand.)

QUANTIFICATION

▲ At the water table, two children scoop up plastic "ice" balls with fish nets and put them into buckets. Tyler says, "You have too many red ones!" Will responds, "I only have three."

▲ In the manipulative area, Darwin spins a spinner and picks up marbles with a melon scoop. He decides how many marbles to take by pointing to the dots on the spinner and taking one marble for each dot.

▲ At the snack table, a group of children take turns serving themselves crackers. Debbie lines up her crackers and counts them. She then counts the crackers on Hazel's napkin. Upon discovering that she has three crackers and Hazel has four, Debbie reaches into the basket and takes one more cracker.

DIVISION OF MATERIALS

▲ In the art area, Michael deals out the playdough implements so that each child at the table has one knife, two cookie cutters, and one roller.

▲ At group time, twenty kindergarten children decide to use three different types of instruments to add interest to a song. A heated discussion occurs as they try to decide how to divide *evenly* the three kinds of instruments among the twenty children.

▲ Liz brings stickers to school to share with the class on her birthday. After she gives one sticker to each child,

Liz still has a handful left. She begins to give one
more sticker to each child, but she does not have
enough stickers for the last two children. "I'll bring
two more tomorrow," Liz says.

Math possibilities abound in whole-math classrooms. Even
more opportunities are created as teachers develop exciting curriculum ideas to replace sterile math materials.

The Whole-Math Child

What is the developmental stage of preschool and kindergarten children?

*Preschool and kindergarten children are in a stage of cognitive
development that Piaget calls "preoperational."[3]* Preoperational children are characterized by extensive language growth that helps
them to solve cognitive problems. However, they are still swayed
in logical thinking by their perceptions. For example, preoperational children usually believe that two rows have the same
number of chips if they are the same length. They do not consider how closely the chips are spaced in the two rows. Perceptual
errors can thus lead preoperational children to make mistakes
when solving mathematical problems.

Young preschool children are egocentric. They tend to view
all questions personally. For example, some young preschoolers
answer all quantification questions by giving their own age. Children become more logical in their thinking as they mature. They
progress through predictable stages of quantification.

What are the developmental stages of quantification?

*Children progress through three stages of quantification: global,
one-to-one correspondence, and counting.[4]*

GLOBAL
Children at this level quantify perceptually. If asked to take as
many counters as are in another group, they may take a
handful or make a pile or row that looks about the same as
the model set.

ONE-TO-ONE CORRESPONDENCE
At this level children attempt to make an equivalent set by
taking one object for each object in the original set. They often point to each object in the first set and take one object for
their new set each time they point, or they may line up the
objects in rows so that each object in the first set is opposite
one object in the second set.

COUNTING

At this stage, children realize that the last number they count is how many they have. This is called *cardinality.* Children decide how many to take by counting the objects in the original set and then counting out an equivalent number of new pieces.

Rochel Gelman and C. R. Gallistel identify the process of saying the number words in a consistent sequence as a necessary aspect of solving problems with counting.[5] This is called *stable order* counting. The child must also understand the necessity of saying one and only one counting word for each object counted. This is an application of the concept of *one-to-one correspondence* to counting.

Children may revert to an earlier stage of quantification as quantities become larger. For example, a child who has stable-order counting to four may use counting to decide how many objects to take when she rolls a three on a die but use one-to-one correspondence when she rolls a six.

Do children make mistakes?

Yes indeed! We all make mistakes, not just in math, but in anything we are learning. We construct knowledge and develop higher-level thinking skills as we attempt to correct our errors.

Quantification mistakes are developmentally appropriate in young children, just as grammatical errors or mispronounced words are typical. Most children make the same types of mistakes over a prolonged period of time as they gradually expand and refine their thinking skills. Rather than being viewed as wrong or right, children's answers provide teachers with valuable insight on each child's current level of thinking and guide the teacher in the formulation of new materials or questioning strategies.

Is whole math appropriate for all children?

Yes. Young children everywhere are holistic learners. They learn most effectively in an atmosphere of acceptance that encourages their natural ability to think. We, as early childhood educators, are challenged to create classrooms in which all children maximize their potential in mathematics. This is done best through whole math.

Normally developing preschool children are autonomous.[6] In other words, they are adamant about asserting themselves and making their own decisions. Adults often consider this characteristic to be annoying, but autonomy is actually vital to the development of mathematical knowledge. The autonomous child will argue about how to solve a problem and will not be easily convinced that another child's solution is correct. Such discussions often result in new learning as children defend and explain their viewpoints. The more compliant child, on the other hand, who may not be as mentally active or as motivated to explore new materials as the autonomous child, may wait for the teacher to solve the problem.

Mathematics requires the examination of problems, actions, materials, and events from different perspectives in order to create logical relationships. Within a math-rich environment, children become flexible in their thinking and are likely to determine non-conventional and creative solutions to problems they encounter. The whole-math classroom not only encourages autonomy, it ultimately requires it.

The Whole-Math Teacher

What is the role of the whole-math teacher?

The whole-math teacher plans the classroom environment, facilitates problem solving, and develops curriculum materials. When interacting with children, she constantly assesses their level of thinking. Then, when the opportunity affords itself, such as when it is the teacher's turn during a game, she can model a level of thinking that is right at or slightly above the child's level.

For example, suppose a child and teacher are playing a game where they take turns spinning a spinner and taking acorns from a bowl. The teacher observes that the child takes a handful of nuts each time he spins and thus appears to be in the global stage of quantification. The teacher might then model the next stage of quantification *when it is her turn.* She could carefully point to each dot on the spinner and take one acorn each time she points. She might even say, "There. I took one acorn for each one of my dots." This may encourage the child to think about the relationship between the quantity of dots and nuts in a new way, if he is close to moving into this level of thinking.

Perhaps the next child to play the game is already using one-to-one correspondence to decide how many acorns to take. With this child, the teacher may model counting to quantify the dots as the teacher takes her turn, since this would be the next level of quantification. The constructivist teacher is constantly observing the thinking levels of each child and modifying her responses accordingly.

What kind of classroom environment does the whole-math teacher provide?

The whole-math teacher creates a well-organized classroom environment in which children feel comfortable making choices among activities. The careful planning that occurs *before* children enter the environment eliminates many classroom management concerns and allows the children and the teacher to concentrate on thinking and problem solving rather than crisis management. (Suggestions for displaying materials in such a way as to minimize management problems are included in each chapter.) In addition, the teacher creates an atmosphere of acceptance where children feel confident enough to risk solving difficult problems without fear of making errors.

How do whole-math teachers encourage children to become problem solvers?

Whole-math teachers encourage children to think and solve problems for themselves by facilitating children's reasoning rather than providing solutions for them. The goal is to develop in children a mind-set that *they* can be the problem solvers. Whole-math teachers recognize that there are many possible methods for solving a problem and that children need the freedom to select their own thinking strategies even if their solutions turn out to be incorrect. When teachers try to impose a particular method for solving a problem, children often give up trying to attack the problem themselves.

Why do whole-math teachers avoid correcting errors?

Whole-math teachers recognize that errors are developmentally appropriate and reveal the child's current level of thinking. Correcting children's mistakes discourages them from attempting to solve problems themselves. Can you remember a teacher saying, "Think again," "Are you sure?" or "Louise got the right answer"? Perhaps you gave up trying to figure out the problem because you assumed that you were wrong and decided there was no reason to keep trying. Maybe you "parroted" what the teacher said or solved the problem in the teacher's way without understanding the underlying concepts. Constance Kamii calls this *surface compliance.*[7] Teachers can avoid creating such reactions by not correcting children's errors, thinking processes, or final products. We want children to have confidence in their abilities as mathematicians.

As teachers interact with children, they often encounter situations that require great restraint. One of the most difficult tasks for most teachers is to be silent at the appropriate time. We get excited by what children do, say, or attempt; we are eager to help the children develop positive self-concepts. Our enthusiasm can cause us, however, to ask too many questions, give too many solutions, and offer too much praise. We need to give children room to think.

What can teachers do when children make mistakes?

Teachers can encourage discussion among children or model correctly when it is their own turn.

When children play math games together, they often correct each other's errors. Sometimes they argue. When children correct each other, they tend to think even more actively about the problem at hand. They may have to re-evaluate their way of thinking as they attempt to justify their way of solving the problem. This is the opposite of what happens when teachers correct children. Children tend to automatically accept what teachers say and then look to them for answers to future problems. This is why constructivist classrooms encourage children to interact with each other. Thinking changes more quickly when children are not working in isolation.

How do whole-math teachers assess children?

Whole-math teachers assess children primarily through observation. In a math-rich environment, assessment opportunities abound. As teachers play games with children, they can extend both learning and assessment possibilities through well-timed statements or questions that may evoke further thinking or responses from the children. Examples of such leading questions are included in the activities.

The teacher's careful observations provide information which then becomes the stimulus for the design of new games and activities or future questions to ask a child. Curriculum planning thus becomes circular. The teacher plans activities, observes and/or interacts with children as they use materials, and records information about their responses. The teacher then plans variations or extensions of the activities based on this information and observes again, thus starting anew the cycle of observation, interaction, recording, and planning.

The teacher's observations may be recorded either anecdotally or on a specifically designed assessment form. Assessment forms can be a useful tool for determining the developmental progress of an individual child or of the whole class in general. Sample assessment forms are included in the appendix.

How do whole-math teachers individualize curriculum?

Whole-math teachers individualize curriculum by redesigning existing materials or creating new activities with the needs and interests of specific children in mind. They also develop an open-ended curriculum that adjusts to many levels of children.

As teachers become skilled at observing and assessing children, they become increasingly aware of children's levels of math knowledge and errors in thinking. They recognize the need to stimulate certain children in order to encourage new reasoning. This knowledge directs the teacher in the creation of individualized materials. In addition, since the manipulatives teachers modify, the collections they create, and the games they develop can all be open-ended, they are self-leveling materials. In other words, individual children can use these materials at their own level of development. This is why we have listed several possible observations that teachers may make for each activity in this book.

How do whole-math teachers develop materials?

Whole-math teachers design materials by combining an awareness of how children construct mathematical knowledge with their own creativity, imagination, and experience. In whole-math classrooms, teacher-developed math materials gradually replace commercial materials or work sheets. For example, a teacher might search the local odd-lots store and emerge with a divided container, rubber bait worms, and ping-pong balls. What is the connection here to the math curriculum? Perhaps this teacher, like many others, has a limited budget but understands the motivating value of unique math materials and gets great satisfaction from designing activities for children. If you entered this teacher's classroom after the shopping trip, you might see the following:

▲ The divided tray is used with a collection of buttons so that children can group them in various ways.

▲ The worms have been added to the sensory table along with clear buckets and fish nets. Children use problem solving to determine the most acceptable division of the "bait."

▲ The ping-pong balls are used to throw at a felt target made of red, yellow, and blue concentric circles. The teacher has added Velcro fasteners to the balls so that they grip the target. Score sheets are accessible nearby, and children use a variety of methods to represent how many balls stick on red, yellow, or blue.

Each of these activities not only provides opportunities for children to construct mathematical knowledge but also encourages children to be autonomous. This is a major focus for the whole-math teacher.

How can this book help teachers develop a math-rich classroom?

The following chapters describe ways in which teachers can begin to create a math-rich atmosphere. We include materials teachers already have available and suggest ways to present them in a more interesting fashion or in combination with other materials to create a more meaningful mathematical experience for children. As you observe your children, we hope you will become excited about the mathematical knowledge the children construct through the use of innovative materials. Their growing excitement may lead you to try even more new materials. Although these ideas require planning in order to become reality in your classroom, the results are well worth the additional effort.

Modified manipulatives, collections for sorting and classification, grid and path games, graphing activities, and gross-motor activities all provide numerous ways to integrate many levels of math concepts into the classroom. In the subsequent chapters you will learn more about the kinds of supplies you need and where to purchase them, how to make or create math materials, questions to ask, and assessment techniques to use as you observe children using teacher-developed materials in your classroom.

ENDNOTES

1. For more information about whole language, see Don Holdaway, *The Foundations of Language* (Sydney: Ashton Scholastic, 1979).

2. For more information about the importance of incorporating real math problems, see National Council of Teachers of Mathematics, *Curriculum and Evaluation Standards for School Mathematics* (Reston, VA: NCTM, 1989).

3. Barry J. Wadsworth, *Piaget's Theory of Cognitive and Affective Development*, 4th ed. (White Plains, NY: Longman, 1989), p. 59.

4. Constance Kamii, *Number in Preschool and Kindergarten* (Washington, DC: NAEYC, 1982), p. 35.

5. Rochel Gelman and C. R. Gallistel, *The Child's Understanding of Number*, 2nd ed. (Cambridge, MA: Harvard University Press, 1986), p. 79.

6. Erik H. Erikson, *Childhood and Society*, 2nd ed. (New York: W. W. Norton & Company, 1963), p. 251.

7. Kamii, p. 43.

CHAPTER 2

Math Manipulatives

What would motivate a teacher to acquire five varieties of ice cube trays? The incentive is the never-ending quest for exciting and appropriate manipulatives that stimulate logical-mathematical thinking. Since the bulk of the commercially available manipulatives are expensive and do not facilitate the construction of mathematical concepts, the task falls to the classroom teacher to develop curriculum materials that will facilitate this construction. Ice cube trays, test tube holders, potpourri pine cones, cloth strawberries, and a vast array of found and purchased goodies will, when carefully assembled by a teacher knowledgeable in how children learn, become a stimulating, ever-challenging curriculum framework. These materials—

- ▲ allow for individualization,
- ▲ coordinate with the overall curriculum,
- ▲ are interesting and motivational, and
- ▲ supply extensive materials for even a low-budget classroom.

Teachers' Questions

What are teacher-made math manipulatives?

Teacher-made math manipulatives are interactive materials teachers design to encourage mathematical thinking and problem solving. The materials channel children's thinking toward math concepts through active play. Teacher-made math manipulatives include manipulative games, flannelboards, teacher-made books, and manipulative pieces to coordinate with *predictable* books or songs. (A predictable book or song has a strong rhyme, rhythm, or repetitive text, which allows children to easily remember or predict the words.)

Why is it important to include math manipulatives in the curriculum?

Manipulative materials allow children to make sets with movable objects. This is an essential component of a developmentally appropriate math curriculum for young children and is not possible with work sheets (Kamii 1982, p. 27). As children work at constructing equivalent sets and comparing sets, they can physically reassemble the objects and observe and contemplate the results.

What makes a good math manipulative?

A good math manipulative encourages children to think about numerical or other mathematical relationships. The manipulative area is a thriving component of developmentally appropriate preschool and kindergarten classrooms. Children love to manipulate materials, so toys with movable pieces, such as pegboards and beads, are popular. Math manipulatives, however, must do more than just encourage children to move pieces around, because mathematics is a mental operation. Children construct mathematical concepts by thinking about relationships such as "more," "less," or "same." A good math manipulative, therefore, must stimulate mathematical thinking.

Well-designed math manipulatives provide physical materials to help children visualize the mathematical procedures they are mentally contemplating. They allow children to experiment cognitively by moving the pieces around and observing the results, which is something that cannot be done in a workbook. Good manipulatives also enable children to use their own thinking strategies, based on their cognitive levels, to solve real math problems.

What is wrong with commercial math manipulatives?

Many commercial manipulative materials merely encourage children to handle the pieces without doing any mathematical reasoning. For example, Unifix stairs have just enough spaces in each column for the correct number of cubes to match the given numeral. All a child need do is fill up the column. There is no need to think about quantity and no motivation to do so. Other manipulatives have pegs to fit in numbered pegboards or beads to place on numbered dowels but are designed so that all the child does is fill up the available space. Since these manipulatives do not promote thinking, they are not really math materials.

What concepts emerge as children play with math manipulatives?

The concepts of one-to-one correspondence and quantification emerge as children attempt to construct equivalent sets. Children are constantly evaluating how many manipulative pieces to take. In the process, their thinking strategies evolve from global to one-to-one correspondence to counting. Some children begin to develop addition and even subtraction skills. Some children also construct concepts of multiplication and division.

How do math manipulatives encourage children to quantify?

Dice or spinners encourage children to quantify with math manipulatives since they must decide how many manipulative pieces to take after they roll the dice or spin the spinner. When young children are asked to construct equivalent sets, they can often handle quantities to three but not higher. For this reason, dice that have only one, two, or three dots per side are appropriate to use with math manipulatives at first. They are referred to as "1-3 dice" throughout the book. Later, dice may be used with up to six dots per side. We call these "1-6 dice."

All of our dice use dots rather than numerals. When young children use dice with dots, they can select a strategy for constructing an equivalent set that is commensurate with their level of thinking. Children at the one-to-one correspondence stage can point to each dot in succession and select a counter for each dot. Children who count to quantify can use that strategy. Numeral dice, on the other hand, limit the problem-solving possibilities of the game. Only children who recognize the numeral and the quantity it represents can play.

What is the easiest way to alter a manipulative material so that it encourages mathematical thinking?

Add dice or a spinner. Adding dice or a spinner immediately infuses a manipulative material with math-rich potential. Instead of just being a pegboard, now it's a math game. Children who have become bored with just manipulating the pieces suddenly become interested in the material again and begin to reason mathematically as they attempt to figure out how many they have on their die or spinner and how many pieces they need to take. If they are playing with another child they may want to find out who rolled the higher quantity, who has more pieces, or how many more pieces they need to catch up. Suddenly, they are comparing sets, quantifying, adding, and subtracting, all because a sterile material was transformed into a game.

How can teachers make dice?

Teachers can make dice with stickers and one-inch cubes. The tiny dots on standard dice are difficult for many young children to point to. Dice made from one-inch cubes, which can accommodate larger circles, solve this problem. Many teachers already have one-inch cubes in their manipulative equipment. Cubes can also be purchased at craft stores. Quarter-inch-round file stickers work well for the dots. Fingernail stickers with bright pictures add variety; puffy stickers help children who need to feel the dot while counting.

When teachers make dice, they can arrange the dots in non-standard configurations. Children may memorize and label the patterns of dots on standard dice without understanding the underlying concept of quantification. Placing the dots in a variety of patterns for each quantity encourages children to actually quantify the sets.

What affects the difficulty of a math manipulative?

The number of dots on the die or spinner or the number of dice used affects the difficulty of manipulative games. Teachers can make a material easier for a particular child or group by reducing the number of dots on the die or spinner. If the material calls for a 1-6 die, change to a 1-3 die. If the material uses two dice, cut back to one die.

Teachers can make a math game more challenging by increasing the quantity of dots on the dice. A 1-3 die can be upgraded to a 1-6 die. For children who are ready to combine quantities, two or even three dice can be used.

Some materials do not use dice, for example the "10 in the Bed" interactive song chart (activity 2.15). Activities such as this can be made easier by decreasing the number of manipulative pieces, perhaps to five or even three. Similarly, an activity such as the song chart "Three Little Bats" (activity 2.14) can be made more difficult by adding more bats.

When should two dice be used?

Once children are consistently quantifying with a 1-6 die, a second die can be introduced. This requires children to combine two sets of dots—in other words, to add. Children usually add the dice together by counting all the dots. Many children eventually remember all of the addition combinations by repeatedly adding dice in games. Initially, many children count the two dice separately. The teacher can model counting all the dots together when it is her turn.

Again, dice with numerals should be avoided. Children have difficulty adding the numerals even when they understand what the numerals represent. In an informal study conducted by the authors, five-year-old children used a die with dots and a die with numerals to play a game. All of the children added the numerals as one, regardless of what the numerals were. Although the children could all identify the numerals and show how many counters they represented, when adding, they treated all numbers as the quantity *one.*

What errors should teachers expect children to make?

Errors in stable-order counting are common. Skipping over objects to be counted or counting the same objects more than once are also typical.

Teachers should not correct these errors. Such corrections undermine children's self-confidence and do not help them to understand the underlying concepts. Children quickly memorize the order of the number words from hearing teachers and children count throughout the day when playing, reading books, or singing. Children stop skipping over or double-counting objects only when they themselves finally realize the absolute necessity of counting each object once and only once. This takes time. Experience fuels our belief that children eventually stop making these errors as their thinking develops. If anything, correcting them seems to slow down the process. They may stop making the error on a particular game only to continue making it in other situations. Some children avoid math materials after they have been corrected. Children who are not corrected, but who are constantly encouraged to think and evaluate, become enthusiastic, confident problem solvers.

What is the teacher's role?

The teacher should observe and assess, model accordingly, and use appropriate questioning strategies to stimulate thinking. Teachers should initially allow children to play with the materials while they observe. At first children may be intrigued with the manipulative and sociodramatic possibilities of the games and need time to explore these outcomes before they become interested in thinking about them mathematically. So it's okay to let the people counters "talk" to each other (activity 2.8) or the dogs hop around the doghouses (activity 2.10). Later, the teacher may encourage a different use of the materials through modeling or questioning.

In order to model appropriately, the teacher must identify the child's thinking strategy and then model at the same level or slightly above *only* when it is his turn. For example, many children use one-to-one correspondence when trying to take the same number of counters as they rolled on the dice. The teacher will observe them point to each dot in succession and take a manipulative piece each time. Based on his observations, the teacher may feel that the child is not yet secure with one-to-one correspondence and needs time to consolidate this level of thinking. He may model the same strategy when it is his turn. On the other hand, if the teacher believes that the child is secure at the current stage and may be ready to move on to a different level of quantification, he may model counting when it is his turn.

The teacher can also use questions to direct children's thinking:

▲ To stimulate more child interest in comparing sets: *Are there more eggs in this nest or this one?* (activity 2.2)

▲ To encourage the child to think about addition: *How many strawberries will you have if you roll a two next time?* (activity 2.1)

▲ To encourage the child to think about subtraction: *How many ducks will you have if one swims away?* (activity 2.21)

What pitfalls should teachers avoid with math manipulatives?

▲ *Do not become so excited about using questioning techniques that you overwhelm the child.* Remember, questions can also be counterproductive if they distract a child who is already thinking about another concept. Children who feel bombarded with questions may get up and leave the game.

▲ *Refrain from correcting children's errors.* Errors are developmentally appropriate and show the child's level of thinking. Use the errors as a guideline for how to model when it is your turn.

▲ *Do not use too many pieces.* They tend to overwhelm younger children, which encourages dumping.

Where can teachers find materials to make math manipulatives?

Look in craft and fabric stores, flea markets, and drug and hardware stores. Collect natural materials such as pebbles, shells, and pine cones. Ask parents for contributions.

How should math manipulatives be displayed?

Most math manipulative materials can be effectively displayed in baskets or on trays in the manipulative area. They can also be highlighted on a math game table. If the container is attractive and the area is uncluttered, children will be more likely to use the material. When several items go together to make one activity, they should all be grouped on a tray so that children are encouraged to use the pieces together. Thus, placing an ice cube tray, a basket of marbles, a melon scoop, and a spinner all on one tray suggests to children that they spin the spinner and use the scoop to put an equivalent number of marbles into the ice cube tray.

How can teachers assess children's math skills through their use of math manipulatives?

Teachers can choose to keep a notebook of anecdotal records or use an observation-based assessment sheet. Two types of assessment forms are included here. They are identical except that one form charts an entire class's use of one material while the other form documents an individual child's use of different math manipulatives throughout the year. The latter form is particularly useful to teachers doing portfolio-based evaluations of children. Both forms rely on observational data. They allow the teacher to quickly record what a child does with the material, what thinking strategies are employed, and what kinds of developmental errors occur.

Figure 2.1 (page 18) provides brief definitions of the terms used on the assessment sheets.

Figure 2.2 (page 19) shows an example of a class assessment form. Note the apparent differences in levels of mathematical thinking among the three children. This shows a typical range of normal mathematical development. (See A.1 in the appendix for a blank class assessment form.)

Figure 2.3 (page 20) shows an example of an individual assessment form. This form documents a change in mathematical thinking over time. Nancy initially constructed equivalent sets to three using one-to-one correspondence. By September 30 she was solving the same mathematical problem using a different strategy, counting. She used her new mathematical reasoning to solve the same type of problem with a new material, an interactive chart, on October 17. By early November Nancy extended her problem solving via counting to sets of four, but she reverted to a global strategy for larger quantities. (See A.2 in the appendix for a blank individual assessment form.)

Figure 2.1 Terms and Definitions

term	definition	example
free play	Imaginative play, not necessarily involving math	A child hops the squirrel counters randomly around the grid board and pretends they are collecting nuts.
makes sets	Attempts to construct sets of a particular quantity	A child rolls the die and takes the same number of counters as dots on the die or moves the same number of spaces along a path (see Chapter 5).
global	Takes a handful, or fills in randomly within boundaries	A child rolls the die and then grabs a handful of counters.
1:1	Uses one-to-one correspondence to take an equivalent amount	A child takes a game piece each time she points to a dot on the die or places one counter on each sticker of a grid game (see Chapter 4).
counts	Uses counting to decide how many to take	A child counts the dots on the die and then counts a corresponding number of game pieces or moves a corresponding number of spaces along a path (see Chapter 5).
stable-order	Says the number words in the correct order	A child counts 1, 2, 3, 4 in the same order each time. After 4, the number words vary: 1, 2, 3, 4, 8, 6; 1, 2, 3, 4, 6, 9; 1, 2, 3, 4, 9, 8.
skips	Skips over some objects when counting	A child points to the stars faster than she counts. * * * * * * * 1 2 3 4 5
re-counts	Counts some objects more than once	A child counts the stars in the first row, then the stars in the second row, and then some from the first row again.
counts all	Combines two dice by counting all the dots	A child counts all the dots on one die and continues counting all the dots on a second die.
adds on	Knows quantity of first set and counts on without re-counting the first set	A child rolls a three and a six. Recognizing the three, she counts on: 4, 5, 6, 7, 8, 9.
combinations	Remembers some addition combinations	Most children remember "doubles" first, for example, $1 + 1 = 2$; $2 + 2 = 4$; $3 + 3 = 6$.

Figure 2.2 Class Assessment Form

Material: 10 in the Bed chart

child	outcome		strategy			errors			addition			comments
	free play	makes sets	global	1:1	counts	stable-order to	skips	re-counts	counts all	adds on	knows comb.	
Mikey	X											Counts when others play. No attempt to make sets.
Anna		X			X		X					
Latoya		X			X							no errors

Figure 2.3 Individual Assessment Form

Child: Nancy

| date | material | outcome | | strategy | | | errors | | | | addition | | | comments |
		free play	makes sets	global	1:1	counts	stable-order to	skips	re-counts	counts all	adds on	knows comb.	
9/15	strawberries and spinner		X to 3		X								
9/30	strawberries and spinner		X to 3			X	3						
10/17	3 bats chart		X to 3			X	3						
11/3	nuts and ice tray		X to 4	X 5 & 6		X to 4	4						Rolls 1-6 die. Makes correct set for 1-4. Puts in handful for 5-6.

Math
Manipulative
Activities

2./ Strawberry Picking Game

Materials
- ▲ 20 to 30 cloth or plastic strawberries
- ▲ 2 vegetable baskets or other small baskets
- ▲ tongs (optional)
- ▲ 1-3 or 1-6 teacher-made die

Child's Level
This game meets the needs of a wide range of children, from those just beginning to quantify to those comparing larger sets.

What to Look For
Children often roll the die to decide how many strawberries to take.

Children playing the game together may compare how many strawberries they each have.

Some children will count to create an equivalent set between the die and strawberries; others will use one-to-one correspondence.

Some children will count to see how many strawberries they have at the end of the game.

Helpful Hint

Remove the tongs if they are so difficult for the children to use that they distract them from thinking about the math.

Modification
Add an additional die and more strawberries for children who are ready to quantify larger sets.

Questions to Extend Thinking
How many strawberries do I get to take?

Who do you think has more strawberries? How can we find out?

Integrated Curriculum Activities
Include the book *Blueberries for Sal* by Robert McCloskey (Viking Press, 1976) in the reading area.

Make fruit salad or fruit shakes with the children as a cooking activity.

Set up a farmer's market in the dramatic-play area.

Add plastic fruit and tongs to water in the sensory table.

2.2 Bird Nests and Eggs

Materials
- ▲ 6 small bird nests
- ▲ 25 to 35 small plastic eggs from craft or party store
- ▲ 1-3 or 1-6 teacher-made die or spinner

Child's Level
This game is ideal for children working on one-to-one correspondence or quantification of small sets. It is also challenging for older children who may attempt to create sets of eggs ranging from 1 to 6.

What to Look For
Children often roll the die to
  decide how many eggs to put
  into each nest.
Some children (especially kindergartners) will try to fill the
  nests in order from 1 to 6.
Some children will put one egg into each nest. They are working
  on the concept of one-to-one correspondence.
Children may put eggs into the nests randomly. The teacher can
  play along and comment about quantities of eggs as she plays.

Modification
Use two dice and more eggs for children ready to add sets together. Switch to smaller eggs so that more will fit in the nests.

Questions to Extend Thinking
Which nest has the fewest eggs?
Do you have enough eggs left to put three in this nest?
Look! I have three eggs in my nest. Does that nest have as many
  eggs as my nest?
How many eggs would be left in this nest if one hatched?

Integrated Curriculum Activities
Include the book *Good-Night Owl* by Pat Hutchins (Macmillan,
  1972) in the reading area.
Set out bird nests in the science area.
Play a nature recording of bird songs.

Helpful Hint

Make sure your nests
are big enough to hold
as many eggs as there
are dots on your die or
spinner. Our first set of
nests held only three
eggs!

2.3 Heart Game

Materials
▲ 2 ice cube trays with heart-shaped holes
▲ heart-shaped ice balls
▲ tongs (optional)
▲ 1-3 teacher-made die

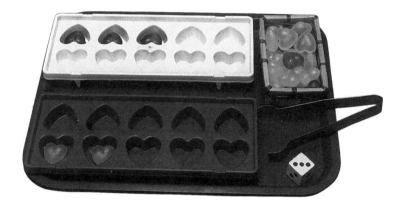

Child's Level
This game is most appropriate for children working on one-to-one correspondence and quantifying small amounts.

What to Look For
Children often roll the die to decide how many hearts to put into their trays.
Some children will count to create an equivalent set between the die and hearts; others will use one-to-one correspondence.
Children may compare how many hearts they each have.
Some children will ignore the die and put one heart into each hole. They are working on one-to-one correspondence.

Helpful Hint

Do not use tongs with very young children. They may be so challenged by manipulating the tongs that they cannot think about the math.

Modification
For more advanced children use smaller hearts, such as heart erasers, and a 1-6 die. Children can put as many hearts as they roll on the die into each compartment of the ice tray and see how many hearts they have at the end of the game.

Questions to Extend Thinking
Who do you think has more hearts?
How many more hearts do you need to fill your tray?
If you roll a one, will you have enough hearts to fill your tray?

Integrated Curriculum Activity
Add a variety of colors and shapes of ice balls, tongs, and buckets to water in the sensory table. Children can sort the ice balls by color or shape as they fish them out of the water.

2.4 Marble Game

Materials
- ▲ 2 ice cube trays with ½-inch round holes
- ▲ enough marbles to fill both trays
- ▲ 2 melon scoops
- ▲ 1 or 2 standard dice (some preschool and many kindergarten children are ready to use two dice)

Child's Level
Since this game has so many marbles (each ice tray holds 60), it is most appropriate for children quantifying to at least six or combining two dice. It is an excellent kindergarten game.

What to Look For
Some children will add the two dice together by counting all the dots.
Some children will count to create an equivalent set between the dice and marbles; others will use one-to-one correspondence.
Some children will ignore the dice and put one marble into each hole. These children are working on one-to-one correspondence.

Modification
Use a third die for children ready to combine three sets.

Questions to Extend Thinking
How can I tell if I have as many marbles as you do?
How many do I need to roll to fill up this row?

Integrated Curriculum Activities
Include a marble track in the manipulative area.
Dip marbles in paint and roll them across paper.
Put ramps in the science area with a variety of objects to roll down them.
Add marbles, ice balls, and clear plastic bottles to water in the sensory table.

Helpful Hints

Use a different color of marble for this game if you have another toy with marbles on the manipulative shelf. This helps the children keep the marbles for the math game separate.

Do not use marbles with young preschoolers who still put things into their mouths.

We used iridescent and metallic marbles because they were intriguing to the children.

2.5 Nature Game

Materials

▲ 2 ice cube trays
▲ small nuts and small pine cones (enough of each to fill one tray)
▲ 2 tongs (optional)
▲ 1-3 teacher-made die or spinner

Child's Level

Since this game has relatively few pieces, it is a good beginning game for children working on one-to-one correspondence or quantification to three.

What to Look For

Children often use the die or spinner to determine how many nuts or pine cones to put into their trays.

Some children will count to create an equivalent set between the die and the nuts or pine cones; others will use one-to-one correspondence.

Children may compare the number of nuts one has with the number of pine cones another has.

Some children will disregard the die or spinner and put one item into each hole. They are working on one-to-one correspondence.

Modification

Change the type of nuts used to add variety.

Questions to Extend Thinking

Are there more nuts or more pine cones in the trays?
How many more pine cones do you need in order to have as many pine cones as nuts?
If you roll a two, will your tray be full?
How many more do you need to fill your tray?

Integrated Curriculum Activities

Include a nut collection (activity 3.15) in the manipulative area.
Set out various types and sizes of pine cones in the science area.
Put large nuts, such as buckeyes, with buckets and tongs in the sensory table.
Take a nature walk.

Helpful Hints

Tiny pine cones can be found in some potpourri mixtures or in some craft stores.

Eliminate the tongs if they distract the children from focusing on quantification, but first allow several days for the novelty of the tongs to wear off.

2.6 Pom-Pom Game

Materials
- ▲ 2 watercolor trays
- ▲ 2 colors of pom-poms (enough of each color to fill one tray)
- ▲ tongs (optional)
- ▲ 1-3 teacher-made die or spinner

Child's Level
This game is most appropriate for children working on one-to-one correspondence or quantification to three.

What to Look For
Children often use the die or spinner and take an equivalent number of pom-poms.

Some children, especially younger ones, will ignore the die or spinner and put one pom-pom into each space on the tray. They are working on one-to-one correspondence.

Children may compare quantities between the two colors of pom-poms.

Some children will count to create an equivalent set between the die and pom-poms; others will use one-to-one correspondence.

Modification
Older children may attempt to create patterns by alternating colors of pom-poms. Add pom-poms in a third color to allow for more complex patterns.

Questions to Extend Thinking
Are there more pink or blue pom-poms in the trays?

How many more pink do you need in order to have as many pink as blue?

How many more do you need to fill your tray?

If I roll a one, will my tray be full?

Integrated Curriculum Activities
Provide colored cotton balls for a collage.

Put colored cotton balls, tongs, and baskets in the sensory table.

Helpful Hints

Watercolor trays come with 6 or 10 compartments. Use 6-compartment trays for younger classes and 10-compartment trays for older ones.

Avoid using cotton balls with math games. Children easily tear them apart.

2.7 Bean Game

Materials

▲ bowl of dried beans (lima, pinto, kidney)
▲ 2 ice cream tasting spoons (to pick up the beans)
▲ 2 small baskets or bowls, one for each player
▲ teacher-made bean spinner
▲ 1-3 teacher-made die

Child's Level

This game is intriguing to children at a variety of levels. Young children may just focus on quantifying to three. Older or more advanced children may try to focus on two things: the type of bean and the quantity. This is more difficult than just considering quantity.

What to Look For

Children may spin the spinner to find out what kind of bean to take and roll the die to find out how many to take. Some children will not yet be able to think about both quantity and type of bean at the same time.

Helpful Hint

You can make the bean spinner by dividing a square of poster board into fourths and gluing on the beans. Insert a one-inch paper fastener through the spinner, then through a small bead, and finally through the poster board to mount the spinner. (The bead allows the spinner to rotate above the beans.)

Modification

Change to a 1-6 die for children who are comfortable focusing on both type of bean and quantity.

Questions to Extend Thinking

Are there more lima beans or pinto beans in your bowl?
How many lima beans will you have if you roll a two?
Who do you think has the most beans? How can we tell?

Integrated Curriculum Activities

Include the book *Growing Vegetable Soup* by Lois Ehlert (Harcourt Brace Jovanovich, 1987) in the reading area.
Make bean soup with the children as a cooking activity.
Provide a variety of beans for a collage.
Plant beans.

2.8 People Game

Materials

- ▲ 2 Styrofoam test tube holders or egg cartons
- ▲ 20 to 30 cylindrical wooden or plastic people
- ▲ 1-3 or 1-6 teacher-made die

Child's Level

This game is appropriate for very young children who are focusing on one-to-one correspondence. It is also well suited for children quantifying to six.

What to Look For

Children often roll the die to determine how many people to take.

Children playing the game together may compare how many people they each have.

Children may group the people by attributes.

Some children may count to find out how many people they have at the end of the game.

Some children will count to create an equivalent set between the die and people; others will use one-to-one correspondence.

Modification

Add an accessory item such as a hat for each person. Children can formulate rules for how many people and how many hats to take.

Questions to Extend Thinking

How many people did you end up with?
How many more people do you need to fill this row?
Do you have more people with or without hats?
Do you have more girls or boys?

Integrated Curriculum Activities

Include the book *Changes Changes* by Pat Hutchins (Macmillan, 1986) in the reading area.

Add a doll house and people to the block area.

Helpful Hints

Wooden people are easy to make. Glue wooden balls onto wooden spools with a glue gun. (Craft stores sell these materials.) Draw faces with paint markers and glue on hair.

Cylindrical commercial people such as Fisher Price figures work well.

2.9 Palm Tree Pegboard Game

Materials
- ▲ 20 to 30 plastic palm trees from party supply store
- ▲ standard small-hole pegboard, lollipop display holder, or Styrofoam square
- ▲ 1-3 or 1-6 teacher-made die

Child's Level
This game is suitable for a wide range of children, from those constructing one-to-one correspondence to those quantifying to six.

What to Look For
Children may roll the die and attempt to put a corresponding number of palm trees on their board.

Some children will count to create an equivalent set between the die and palm tree counters; others will use one-to-one correspondence.

If two children are playing, they may compare quantities of palm trees.

Some children will count to find out how many palm trees they have at the end of the game.

Helpful Hint

Trim the bottom of bendable plastic palm trees to fit your pegboard.

Modification
Add a second die for more advanced children.

Questions to Extend Thinking
How many palm trees do you have so far?
Do I have as many palm trees as you do?
How many more palm trees do you need to fill your pegboard?

Integrated Curriculum Activities
Include the book *Chicka Chicka Boom Boom* by Bill Martin, Jr., and John Archambault (Simon & Schuster, 1989) in the reading area.
Put a variety of coconuts in the science area. Let the children guess what is inside, and then open them.
Use hollow coconut half-shells as instruments in the music area.
Use hollow coconut half-shells as scoops in the sensory table.
Include the Palm Tree grid game (activity 4.14) as a math activity.

2.10 Doghouse Game

Materials

- ▲ 6 doghouses made from half-pint milk cartons covered with contact paper, with 1 to 6 dots on the roofs
- ▲ small plastic dogs
- ▲ 1-6 die

Child's Level

This game is most appropriate for children quantifying to six, but younger children also find mathematical uses.

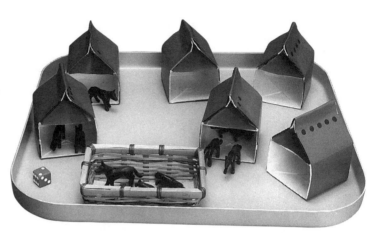

What to Look For

Some children will put as many dogs into a doghouse as they rolled on the die.

Some children will put one dog into each doghouse.

Some children may put a dog into the doghouse whose dots correspond to the quantity they rolled on the die.

Modification

Change the dogs to people or cars to add variety.

Questions to Extend Thinking

Which doghouse should this dog go into?

How did you decide where to put your dog?

How many dogs can live in this doghouse?

Helpful Hint

Ask parents or your school cafeteria to save the milk cartons.

Integrated Curriculum Activities

Include the books *Harry the Dirty Dog* by Gene Zion (Harper and Row, 1956) and *Benjy's Doghouse* by Margaret Bloy Graham (Harper and Row, 1973) in the reading area.

Set up a pet shop in the dramatic-play area.

Sing the traditional song "B-I-N-G-O."

2.11 Shape Sorter Game

Materials
- ▲ commercial 4-compartment shape sorter
- ▲ teacher-made 1-3 die
- ▲ teacher-made color or shape die to match the shape sorter

Child's Level
Younger children will view this material as a shape sorter. The dice add a mathematical challenge for older children ready to focus on two attributes.

What to Look For
Some children will be able to focus only on color (or shape) or quantity, but not both.
Some children will focus on both color (or shape) and quantity. For example, if they roll three dots on one die and the color red on the other, they will take three red pieces.
Some children will vacillate between focusing on color and quantity.

Helpful Hint

Be sure the stickers on your 1-3 die are not the same color as any of the stickers on the color die. This might confuse the children.

Modification
Remove the color die if children have trouble focusing on both number and color. Children can then roll just the dot die and take the corresponding amount of whatever shape they choose.

Questions to Extend Thinking
Do you have just as many blue pieces as red ones?
Which color do you have the most of?
How many more green do you have than red?
If you roll one green, will you have as many green as red?

Integrated Curriculum Activities
Include the book *Changes Changes* by Pat Hutchins (Macmillan, 1986) in the reading area.
Plan a sponge-painting activity with sponges of different shapes.
Add colored wooden blocks to the manipulative or block area.

2.12 Clothespin Game

Materials
- ▲ clothespin and note clips collection (from activity 3.6)
- ▲ 2 racks (shelf extenders) for the clothespins and clips
- ▲ 1-3 or 1-6 die

Child's Level
This game is appropriate for children on many levels, from those using global quantification strategies to those counting to form equivalent sets to six.

What to Look For
Children may use the die to determine how many clothespins to clip onto their rack.

Children may compare how many clothespins are on the two racks.

Some children may count to see how many clothespins they have at the end of the game.

Some children will count to create an equivalent set between the die and clothespins; others will use one-to-one correspondence.

Modification
Add a second die and more clothespins for children who are ready to combine two dice.

Questions to Extend Thinking
Which row has the most clothespins?
Do you have more pink or blue clothespins?
Which rack has the most clothespins? How can we tell?
How many more clothespins are in this row than this one?

Integrated Curriculum Activities
Include the book *The Wind Blew* by Pat Hutchins (Macmillan, 1974) in the reading area.
Dramatize the "Shirt" song from the recording *Make Believe in Movement* by Maya Doray (Kimbo Educational, 1976).
Wash baby clothes and hang them up to dry.
Add a drying rack and pretend washing machine to the dramatic-play area.

Helpful Hint

Any of the collections (chapter 3) can be made into quantification games by adding a die or spinner.

2.13 Marble Can Addends Game

Materials

▲ 6 tuna fish cans, spray-painted and mounted on wood
▲ a sponge piece glued to the bottom of each can to partially divide it
▲ round stickers (¼-inch) attached to the wood in consecutive quantities from 1 to 6
▲ 21 marbles

Child's Level

This game is intended for kindergarten children who are beginning to focus on what combinations equal a particular sum. Younger children, however, may enjoy deciding how many marbles to put into the cans.

What to Look For

Children often use the dots on the wood to determine how many marbles to put into each can.

Children may roll the marbles around in the cans and observe the different configurations.

Older children may focus on the different groupings that add up to the same total. (Some of our kindergarten children wrote down such combinations. This was their idea, not ours.)

Helpful Hints

Be sure to file the edges of the cans so they are not sharp.

Do not use marbles with young preschoolers who still put things into their mouths.

Modification

Supply paper and pencil for children who become interested in notating the various combinations. Let them use whatever notation system they devise, whether it be slash marks, circles, or numerals, since this will have meaning for them.

Questions to Extend Thinking

Which can has the most marbles?
How did you decide how many marbles to put into each can?
What happens when you roll the marbles around? Are there still the same number of marbles in the can?
How many marbles are on each side of the can? How many marbles are there all together?

Integrated Curriculum Activities

Include a marble track in the manipulative area.
Dip marbles in paint and roll them across paper.
Put ramps in the science area with objects to roll down them.
Add marbles, ice balls, and clear plastic bottles to water in the sensory table.

2.14 "Three Little Bats" Interactive Song Chart

Predictable Song
"Three Little Bats" (see B.1 in the appendix for the music)

Materials
- ▲ interactive chart (as pictured) made of poster board and laminated
- ▲ movable bat pieces made of felt and attached to the chart with magnetic tape

Child's Level
This activity is most appropriate for young preschoolers who are counting or quantifying to three.

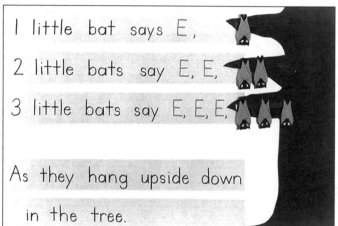

I little bat says E,

2 little bats say E, E,

3 little bats say E, E, E,

As they hang upside down

in the tree.

What to Look For
Some children will put one, two, or three bats on the appropriate lines of the chart to match the song words.
Children often discuss how many bats to put on the chart.
Children may correct each other.
Some children will count the bats.

Modification
Add more bats and movable numeral cards to extend the song to six.

Questions to Extend Thinking
Which row has the most bats?
How did you decide how many bats to put here?
What would happen if one more bat came?
What would happen if one bat flew away?

Integrated Curriculum Activities
Include the book *Stellaluna* by Janell Cannon (Harcourt Brace, 1993) in the reading area.
Let children dramatize the song.

Helpful Hint

When we first made the chart we were thinking about whole language and not math. The chart already had the correct number of places to hang the bats, so the children did not have to think about quantification. We remade the chart with magnetic strips so that the children would have to decide how many bats to put on the chart.

2.15 "10 in the Bed" Interactive Song Chart

Predictable Book or Song
"10 in the Bed" (traditional counting song)
There Were Ten in the Bed (predictable book) by Pam Adams (Child's Play, 1991) or *Ten Bears in My Bed* (predictable book) by Stan Mack (Pantheon Books, 1974)

Materials
▲ chart (as pictured) made of poster board and laminated
▲ 10 felt teddy bears backed with poster board
▲ numeral cards, 1-10, with magnetic tape, to attach to the chart

Child's Level
This game is most appropriate for older preschool or kindergarten children who are counting or quantifying to ten.

What to Look For
Children often place the bears on the chart and remove them as they sing.
Some children will coordinate the number of bears on the chart with the numeral and the words of the song.
Children may debate how many bears to put on the chart or whether the correct number of bears is on the chart.
Some children will be able to quantify with small numbers but not larger ones.

Modification
Reduce the number of bears to five if ten are too many.

Questions to Extend Thinking
How many bears will be in the bed if one falls out? If two fall out?
What would happen if one bear got back in?

Integrated Curriculum Activities
Include the books *Golden Bear* by Ruth Young (Viking Press, 1992), *Ira Sleeps Over* by Bernard Waber (Houghton Mifflin, 1972), and *Corduroy* by Don Freeman (Viking Press, 1968) in the reading area.
Provide a wooden doll house bed and small people or bears (activity 2.19) so children can re-enact the song.
Include the teddy bear path games (activities 5.3 and 5.14) as math activities, if appropriate for your group.
Add teddy bear pasta to the art area.
Use teddy bear crackers for snack.

There were 5 in the bed
And the little one said,
"Roll over! Roll over!"
So they all rolled over
And one fell out!

Helpful Hint
The felt teddy bears can be cut out with an Elison machine if a piece of paper is put underneath the felt.

2.16 Trick or Treat Interactive Chart

Predictable Book

Where's the Halloween Treat? by Harriet Ziefert (Viking Penguin, 1985)

Materials

- ▲ interactive chart with a door to open (as pictured) made from poster board and laminated
- ▲ small, laminated pictures of the treats in the book
- ▲ numeral cards to attach to the chart

Child's Level

This game is most appropriate for children quantifying to six.

What to Look For

Many children will follow along with the book as they use the chart. Some children will count to create an equivalent set between the die and trick-or-treat counters; others will use one-to-one correspondence to decide how many pictures to put on the chart. Children often debate how many pieces to put on the chart and correct each other.

Modification

Some children may wish to make new trick-or-treat pieces for the chart. They will have to decide how many pieces of each treat they will need.

Questions to Extend Thinking

Which treat is there the most of?
Which treat is there the fewest of?
Are there enough oranges for six people?

Integrated Curriculum Activities

Include the book *The Humbug Witch* by Lorna Balian (Abingdon Press, 1965) in the reading area.
For a cooking activity, make muffins or popcorn, as in the book.

Helpful Hints

Attach a clear pocket made from extra laminating film to the chart to hold the treats, or use magnetic tape.

Make more of each treat than are in the book so that the children must decide how many to take in order to re-enact the story.

2.17 "5 Little Monkeys" Finger Puppets

Predictable Finger Play
"5 Little Monkeys" (traditional)

Materials
▲ 5 teacher-made felt finger puppets, as pictured

Child's Level
This game is appropriate for many levels, from young children focusing on one-to-one correspondence to children quantifying to five or thinking about subtraction.

What to Look For
Children usually place one monkey on each finger in one-to-one correspondence.
Some children will find it easier to remove one puppet at a time than to hold down a finger, as is usually done in the finger play.
Some children will requantify each time they remove a puppet to see how many are left.
Some children will be able to subtract by one.

Helpful Hint

Make the puppets' eyes from felt or with a permanent marker. Wobbly eyes fall off easily.

Modifications
Reduce the number of monkeys to three if five are too many.
Increase the number of monkeys to ten if five are too few.

Questions to Extend Thinking
How many monkeys are left?
How many monkeys will you have if two fall off?
How many monkeys will you have if you put one back on your finger?

Integrated Curriculum Activities
Include the book *Caps for Sale* by Esphyr Slobodkina (Addison-Wesley, 1968) in the reading area.
Read the big book *Five Little Monkeys Jumping on the Bed* by Eileen Christelow (The Trumpet Club, 1989) with the children.
Have children dramatize the poem.
Add zoo animals to the block area.
Include the "5 Little Monkeys" manipulative game (activity 2.18) in the manipulative or block area.

2.18 "5 Little Monkeys" Manipulative Game

Predictable Finger Play
"5 Little Monkeys" (traditional)

Materials
▲ 5 small monkeys
▲ wooden doll house bed

Child's Level
This game is most appropriate for children quantifying to five or children interested in subtraction.

What to Look For
Children often place the monkeys onto the bed and remove one monkey each time they sing a verse.

Many children will have to re-count to see how many monkeys are left on the bed each time they remove one.

Some children will subtract by one mentally, especially after repeated experiences with the game.

Some children will be able to visually identify one, two, or three monkeys without counting.

Children often discuss and debate how many monkeys are on the bed.

Modifications
Reduce the number of monkeys to three if five are too many.
Increase the number of monkeys to ten if five are too few.

Questions to Extend Thinking
How many monkeys would be left on the bed if two fell off?
How many monkeys would be on the bed if one got back on?

Integrated Curriculum Activities
Include the book *Caps for Sale* by Esphyr Slobodkina (Addison-Wesley, 1968) in the reading area.
Read the big book *Five Little Monkeys Jumping on the Bed* by Eileen Christelow (The Trumpet Club, 1989) with the children.
Add zoo animals to the block area.
Include "5 Little Monkeys" finger puppets (activity 2.17) in the manipulative or block area.

Helpful Hints

We used pieces from a rubber puzzle for the monkeys.

Pieces from commercially available "Barrel of Monkeys" games also work well.

2.19 "10 in the Bed" Manipulative Game

Predictable Song or Book
"10 in the Bed" (traditional counting song)
There Were Ten in the Bed (predictable book) by Pam Adams
(Child's Play, 1991) or *Ten Bears in My Bed* (predictable book)
by Stan Mack (Pantheon Books, 1974)

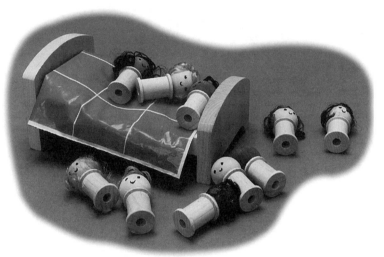

Materials
▲ 10 small teddy bears or people
▲ wooden doll house bed

Child's Level
This game is most appropriate for children who are quantifying to ten, although other children often watch and model or play with the pieces in their own way.

What to Look For
Children often place the figures on the bed and remove one each time they sing a verse.
Many children will need to re-count to see how many figures are left on the bed each time one is removed.
Some children will subtract by one mentally, especially after they reach the smaller quantities.
Children will discuss and debate how many figures are on the bed.

Helpful Hint

Ten is a fairly large quantity for many preschool children. Expect some serious disagreements about how many bears (or people) are left in the bed!

Modifications
Reduce the number of figures to five if ten are too many.
Younger children who are still working on stable-order counting may need a song that counts forward rather than backward. You can change the words of the song to—

There was one in the bed and the little one said,
"I'm lonely, I'm lonely."
So he rolled over and one climbed in.
There were two in the bed….

Questions to Extend Thinking
How many bears (or people) will there be if one climbs back in?
How many bears (or people) will be left if two fall out?

Integrated Curriculum Activities

Include the books *The Napping House* by Audrey Wood
(Harcourt Brace Jovanovich, 1984), *The Cuddlers* by Stacy
Towle Morgan (La Leche League International, 1993), and
K is for Kiss Good Night by Jill Sardegna (Doubleday, 1994) in the
reading area.

Include the "10 in the Bed" interactive song chart (activity 2.15)
as a whole-language activity.

Put plastic people or small plush teddy bears in the block area.
Children may make a bed out of blocks and use the people or
teddy bears to act out the song.

2.20 Caterpillar Manipulative Game

Predictable Book
The Very Hungry Caterpillar by Eric Carle (Putnam, 1969)

Materials
▲ plastic fruits to correspond to those in the book, but include more than enough pieces of each fruit so that the children have to figure out how many of each they need to re-enact the story
▲ small toy caterpillar—available commercially, or make a caterpillar out of pom-poms

Child's Level
This game is most appropriate for children who are quantifying to five.

Helpful Hint

Do not include the additional foods in the book. They may confuse children who are trying to quantify the fruits.

What to Look For
Children often attempt to re-enact the story by taking the appropriate amount of each fruit.

Some children will count and some children will use one-to-one correspondence in order to take the amount of each type of fruit used in the story.

Children may discuss how much of each fruit to take.

Some children will be able to take one, two, or three pieces without counting.

Some children will select the fruit in the same order as in the book but will take all of the available pieces of each fruit.

Modification
Kindergarten children may enjoy rewriting the book to include sets of fruits to ten.

Questions to Extend Thinking

Which fruit did the caterpillar eat the most of?

Which fruit did he eat the least of?

Which fruit would you eat the most of? How many pieces would you eat?

How many pears are left over?

Integrated Curriculum Activities

Read the big book *The Very Hungry Caterpillar* (Scholastic, 1989) with the children.

Create word cards with illustrations to match the fruits in the book for the writing center.

Make fruit salad with the children as a cooking activity.

Add plastic fruits and tongs to water in the sensory table.

Set up a farmer's market in the dramatic-play area.

2.21 "Five Little Ducks" Manipulative Game

Predictable Song
"Five Little Ducks" (traditional song)

Materials
▲ 5 small rubber ducks and one mother duck, placed in a basket or on a bench

Child's Level
Mathematically, this activity is best suited to children who are beginning to count or quantify to five or are interested in subtraction. Of course, very young preschoolers love singing the song and playing with the ducks.

What to Look For
Children will manipulate the ducks as they sing the familiar song.
Children may subtract one duck for each verse.
Many children will have to re-count to see how many ducks are left each time one is subtracted.
Some children will subtract one mentally.
Children may discuss and debate how many ducks are left.

Helpful Hint

You can make the song into a book by using duck stickers (activity 2.24).

Modifications
Reduce the number of ducks to three if five are too many.
Increase the number of ducks to ten if five are too few.

Questions to Extend Thinking
How many ducks should come back?
What if two ducks forgot to come back? How many would be left?

Integrated Curriculum Activities
Include the book and tape *Five Little Ducks* by Raffi (Crown Publishers, 1989) and the book *Have You Seen My Duckling?* by Nancy Tafuri (Greenwillow Books, 1984) in the reading area.
Have children dramatize the song at group time.
Use duck cookie cutters with paint to make prints at the easel.
Use duck cookie cutters with playdough.
Add a duck rubber stamp to the writing table.
Make duck finger puppets.
Add rubber ducks and nets to water in the sensory table.

2.22 Animal Flannelboard

Predictable Book
1 Hunter by Pat Hutchins (Mulberry Books, 1982)

Materials
- ▲ felt cutouts of the animals in the book or paper cutouts of the animals, laminated or contacted, with Velcro tabs on the backs
- ▲ flannelboard

Child's Level
This game is most appropriate for older preschool or kindergarten children who are quantifying to ten.

What to Look For
Children often follow along with the book as they place the appropriate flannelboard pieces onto the board.

Children may discuss how many there are of each animal.

If there are more than the exact number needed for each animal, children will have to figure out how many to put on the board.

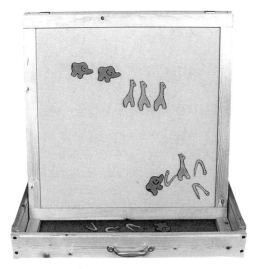

Pictured flannelboard available from Center Concepts, Incorporated, 2414 Ashland Avenue, Cincinnati, Ohio 45206

Modification
Kindergarten children may wish to extend the story by creating larger sets of additional animals.

Questions to Extend Thinking
Are there more giraffes or ostriches?

Which animal is there the most of?

Which animal is there the fewest of?

How many more giraffes are there than elephants?

Integrated Curriculum Activities
Include the book *Dear Zoo* by Rod Campbell (Four Winds Press, 1982) in the reading area.

Add zoo animals to the block area.

Set up a zoo nursery in the dramatic-play area, perhaps with plush animals, white jackets, stethoscopes, and baby bottles.

Helpful Hints

Questions involving set comparisons should be with small sets (one to four). Young children are often overwhelmed by larger quantities.

Wrapping paper is a good source of zoo animal cutouts.

2.23 Pretzel Magnetic Board

Predictable Song
"Salty Pretzels" (see B.2 in the appendix for the words and music)

Materials
▲ magnetic board or cookie sheet
▲ 10 or more pretzel magnets
▲ magnetic numerals to 4 (optional)

Child's Level
This game is most appropriate for children working on stable-order counting or quantification to four.

What to Look For
Children may add pretzels to the magnetic board to correspond with the numbers in the song.
Children may debate how many pretzels to put on the board for each line of the song.

Modification
Add additional verses to the song for children ready to count beyond 4 pretzels to 8 or 12.

Questions to Extend Thinking
How can we tell how many pretzels to put on the board?
How many more pretzels do we need if there are six children and they each want one?

Integrated Curriculum Activities
Include the "Salty Pretzel" teacher-made book (activity 2.25) in the reading area.
Set up a bakery in the dramatic-play area.
Make soft pretzels with the children as a cooking activity.

Helpful Hints

You can purchase pretzel magnets or make them out of dough.

You can also laminate paper cutouts of pretzels and put magnetic tape on the backs.

2.24 "Five Little Ducks" Counting Book

Predictable Song
"Five Little Ducks" (traditional counting song)

Materials
▲ teacher-made book (as pictured) made of duck stickers mounted on green construction paper and laminated

Child's Level
This game is most appropriate for children quantifying to five.

Five little ducks
Went out to play
Over the hills
And far away
    Mother duck said,
    "Quack, quack, quack"

What to Look For
Children often follow the book as they sing the song.
Some children will have to re-count to see how many ducks came back.
Children may discuss how many ducks are left.
Many children will recognize one, two, or three ducks without counting.

Modifications
Reduce the number of ducks to three if five are too many.
Increase the number of ducks to ten for children who are ready.

Questions to Extend Thinking
How many ducks came back?
How can you tell how many ducks came back?
What would happen if two ducks forgot to come back?

Integrated Curriculum Activities
Include the books *Five Little Ducks* by Raffi (Crown Publishers, 1989) and *Have You Seen My Duckling?* by Nancy Tafuri (Greenwillow Books, 1984) in the reading area.
Have children dramatize the song at group time.
Use duck cookie cutters with paint to make prints at the easel.
Use duck cookie cutters with playdough.
Add a duck rubber stamp to the writing table.
Make duck finger puppets.
Add rubber ducks and nets to water in the sensory table.

Helpful Hint

Be sure to neatly print the words to the song exactly as the children sing it, since this also makes an excellent whole-language activity.

2.25 "Salty Pretzel" Counting Book

Predictable Song
"Salty Pretzels" (see B.2 in the appendix for the words and music)

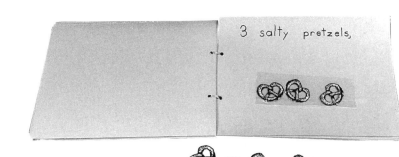

3 salty pretzels,

Materials
▲ pretzel drawings
▲ pretzel cutouts, laminated or contacted
▲ orange (or other desired color) construction paper
▲ marker
▲ lamination

Description
Write the song twice in the book with one line of the song per page. The first time through, use pretzel drawings to illustrate the appropriate numbers of pretzels from the song. The second time through, place a blank pocket made from extra laminating film on each page. The children must decide how many pretzel cutouts to put into each pocket. This encourages quantifying as well as counting.

Child's Level
This game is most appropriate for children working on counting or quantification to four.

What to Look For
Children often follow the book as they sing the song.
Some children will count the pretzels on each page.
Children may discuss how many pretzel cutouts to put into the pockets.
Some children will recognize one, two, or three pretzels without counting.

Modifications
Kindergarten children may want to make their own salty pretzel books and decide how many pretzels to use.
Children may wish to change the words to "yummy cookies," "juicy oranges," etc.

Helpful Hint

Be sure to print the words to the song exactly as the children sing it. Some children will point to the words as they sing.

Questions to Extend Thinking

How many pretzels should go into this pocket?
How did you decide how many pretzels should go on this page?
How many pretzels would we have if we baked one more?

Integrated Curriculum Activities

Include the pretzel magnetic board game (activity 2.23) in the
    manipulative area.
Set up a bakery in the dramatic-play area.
Make soft pretzels with the children as a cooking activity.

2.26 Cookie Sharing Manipulative Game

Predictable Book
The Doorbell Rang by Pat Hutchins (Greenwillow Books, 1986)

Materials
▲ 12 small people figures for the book characters
▲ 12 discs to represent the cookies (marble chips, small bottle caps, circles cut from plastic lids, or tiny eraser cookies)

Child's Level
This is a challenging book extension and is most appropriate for kindergarten children or advanced preschoolers.

What to Look For
Children may use the discs and people figures to act out the quantification and division problems that emerge from the story.

Expect many different strategies to emerge as the children divide the cookies.

Many children will not arrive at a solution, or at least a correct solution; they may, however, continue to mull over the problem and attempt it again later.

Some children may align the people and "cookies" in one-to-one correspondence.

Modification
Teachers may wish to ask older kindergartners or first graders who are confident at dividing or redividing the twelve cookies what could be done if there were only six cookies!

Questions to Extend Thinking
The math problems posed by the book are very challenging. We would not introduce any additional questions for this game.

Integrated Curriculum Activities
Use cookie cutters with playdough.

Make chocolate chip cookies and allow children in small groups to figure out how to divide them.

Set up a bakery in the dramatic-play area.

Helpful Hints

You may want to demonstrate re-enacting the story with the manipulative pieces at group time before putting them on the shelf. Try to foster group discussion and solicit many ideas as the children tell *you* how to divide the cookies.

Resist the urge to tell or show the children how to divide the cookies. Your goal should be to encourage the children to be the problem solvers.

2.27 Recycling Collection Game *Idea by Cathy Hudson*

Materials

- ▲ poster board, 15 by 15 inches
- ▲ illustration of nature scene
- ▲ 25 to 50 assorted small counters such as pop cans, Styrofoam boxes, and newspapers found at novelty or party stores
- ▲ 2 small trash cans (6 inches high)
- ▲ 1-6 die

Child's Level

This game is most appropriate for older preschool and kindergarten children who can quantify to at least six.

Keep the environment clean.

What to Look For

Children may roll the die and take a corresponding amount of trash to put into their trash cans.

Some children may sort the trash into groups by attributes such as type, size, or material.

Children may collect trash in the cans and dump it onto the board.

Some children may count or compare quantities of different types of trash.

Modifications

Reduce the number of pieces of trash if the original amount is too overwhelming.

Kindergarten children may wish to graph the trash they collect.

Questions to Extend Thinking

How do you know which trash to clean up first?

Did you clean up equal amounts of cans and newspapers?

How many more pieces of trash are left to clean up?

Did you each pick up the same amount of trash?

Integrated Curriculum Activities

Include the book *Long Live Earth* by Maighan Morrison (Scholastic, 1993) in the reading area.

Clean up trash on the playground or during a neighborhood walk.

Set up a recycling center in the dramatic-play area.

Helpful Hint

Cut newspaper into one-inch pieces and fold or crush to form collection pieces.

ANECDOTE 1

It was the beginning of the school year, and June (age 5) was especially intrigued with the interactive chart that went with the song "10 in the Bed" (activity 2.15). June had no idea how to decide how many bears to put onto the chart. Although she could rote count, she had not yet constructed cardinality. June therefore could not answer the question, "How many do you have?"

June watched intently, day after day, as other children put bears onto the chart, counted to see how many bears there were, and argued with one another over the results. She listened as each child pointed and re-counted to justify her results. Within two weeks June was also counting bears as she placed the appropriate number onto the chart to correlate with the number in the song. June had constructed the important concept of cardinality in only two weeks with no direct teaching, no teacher-made corrections, and no teacher praise or reinforcement.

ANECDOTE 2

Mollie (age $4\frac{1}{2}$) and her teacher were playing a game with a shape sorter, a color die, and a 1-3 die. When it was her turn, Mollie would roll both dice and quickly take the appropriate quantity of shapes in the color she had rolled. Mollie soon became bored.

"Let's change the rules," she said. "From now on, you take two for every dot you roll."

Mollie continued to play the game. She paused for thought after each roll and then took two shapes when she rolled one dot, four shapes when she rolled two dots, and six when she rolled three dots.

Because she was able to express her autonomy by altering the rules of the game, Mollie found a way to make it intellectually challenging. Research shows that when they are not being evaluated (or corrected), children select more difficult mathematical problems to think about (David L. Martin, "Your Praise Can Smother Learning," in *Learning,* Feb. 1977, p. 44).

ANECDOTE 3

Matthew and Jason (both $4\frac{1}{2}$ years old) used a standard 1-6 dot die to play a strawberry-picking game (activity 2.1). The boys took turns rolling the die, counting the dots, and putting an equivalent number of cloth strawberries into their baskets. When the teacher joined them, five strawberries were left in the central game bowl. Matthew rolled four dots and collected four strawberries. He looked at the one remaining strawberry and said with disappointment, "Now Jason will win." Apparently Matthew reasoned that since Jason would get the last strawberry, Jason would end up with one more.

The teacher asked how they could find out if Jason had more. Both boys spontaneously began to count their strawberries. Jason accurately counted his thirteen strawberries and announced the result. Matthew skipped over some and double-counted others but stopped counting when he reached eleven. "Aw, Jason won," he exclaimed.

In the meantime, Jason had re-counted his strawberries and counted only eleven. He accused Matthew of taking two of his strawberries. The teacher again asked how they could find out how many each boy had. Both boys decided to count again. Matthew again skipped over some strawberries and double-counted some, but this time he ended up with fourteen. Matthew was now all smiles. Jason accurately counted his again, but this time only had eleven. He then spotted two strawberries on the floor which he added to his pile. Jason began counting all over again and this time counted thirteen strawberries. Matthew exclaimed, "I have more." Jason looked confused.

The teacher then asked, "Is there another way to find out if you have the same number of strawberries or if one person has more?" Both boys lined up their strawberries across from each other on the table; neither boy, however, attempted to align the strawberries in one-to-one correspondence, so both rows appeared to be the same length. Matthew left the table with satisfaction as he said, "We have the same." Jason stared at the two rows and said, "Well, maybe I have one more than he does."

Although no final correct answer emerged from this lengthy interchange, both boys stretched their thinking as they searched for a solution to the problem. The teacher encouraged them to continue thinking without providing any solutions or evaluations. Although they may not have arrived at the correct answer this time, both boys showed extensive numeracy development, which they used to attempt to solve a difficult math problem.

CHAPTER 3

Collections

Did you ever spend a quiet morning playing with your mother's jewelry box? Perhaps you put all the bracelets together into one pile, all the rings into another, and the earrings into yet a third. Later, maybe you rummaged through again and grouped all your mom's blue jewelry together, all the red jewelry together, and all the gold together. Or maybe you put all the jewelry you liked the best into one pile, the jewelry you "sort of" liked into another, and the jewelry you didn't like much at all into yet a third. As the time slipped away, you were sorting and resorting your mom's jewelry collection, and you were thinking intently about how to group that jewelry.

Children are intrigued with the classification of materials. If you didn't find a jewelry box to rummage through, perhaps you found a button box, or a drawer full of stamps, or Dad's tackle box. As you played with the materials, grouping and regrouping them, you were developing thinking skills underlying such important mathematical concepts as set construction, similarities, and differences, and you were learning how to think about things in more than one way. Collections are introduced into the classroom to provide children with the opportunity to experiment with sorting and classification and to help them develop flexible thinking.

Teachers' Questions

What is a collection?

A collection is a group of intriguing objects for children to sort and classify by various attributes.

Why is it important to include collections in the math curriculum?

Collections encourage children to carefully observe similarities and differences in the attributes of objects, to make many comparisons, and to construct relationships among objects. Collections also help children become more flexible in their thinking and begin to take another person's perspective.

As children play with the objects in collections, they make note of distinguishing features such as color, size, shape, texture, ornamentation, and detail. They then begin to compare objects within the collections, look for similarities or differences, and group them accordingly. This construction of relationships, such as "same," "different," "more," and "less," provides a framework for all later mathematical understanding. Children need ample opportunities to construct these relationships. In *Number in Preschool and Kindergarten* (NAEYC, 1982; p. 26) Constance Kamii emphasizes this importance: "A child who thinks actively in his own way about all kinds of objects and events, including quantities, will inevitably construct number."

Collections encourage children to become more flexible in their thinking. There is no predetermined, correct way to sort the objects. The goal is for children to find a variety of ways to group the materials. Thus, a child playing with a key collection might initially separate all the brass keys from the silver keys. On another day, she might focus on the number or type of holes in the keys, while at a later time she might sort them by size.

Collections can help children take another person's perspective. Young children are egocentric. They assume everyone thinks the same way they do. As children discuss or argue about how to group the items in a collection, they become aware that different people view the same objects in different ways. This helps them move away from such an egocentric viewpoint.

What makes a good collection?

A good collection is highly interesting to young children and can be sorted in several ways. Look for—

▲ objects that are intriguing to young children;

▲ objects that share at least three attributes, such as color, shape, size, or detail, so that they can be sorted in several different ways;

▲ objects that coordinate with the overall curriculum, such as a snowflake collection to go along with a winter theme; and

▲ an appropriate number of objects, so that children have enough to make many cross comparisons, yet are not overwhelmed.

What is wrong with commercial collections?

Commercial collections often have only one or two attributes. Thus, a child might be able to sort a set of teddy bears only by color. This does not encourage the flexible thinking that develops when children can group and regroup objects by several different attributes.

Many commercial collections are the standard, didactic shapes or cubes. Children have often seen this type of material many times and do not find such collections nearly as interesting as Grandma's buttons.

What math concepts emerge when children use collections?

Children develop the ability to sort and classify by multiple attributes. They begin to realize that the same object can be part of more than one set. For example, a particular bottle cap might fit into the green group but also the flip-top group. In addition, children often compare sets to see which has the most items, so collections may encourage quantification and set comparisons. Children may wonder how many more of one type of object they need in order to have as many as are in another group. This invites contemplation of subtraction.

Collection activities encompass a wide developmental range of thinking, which encourages children who are just beginning to sort as well as children who sort by many attributes and quantify the results. Therefore, the "Child's Level" on the activity sheets in this chapter reflect a broad range of development.

What are the easiest collections to begin with?

Keys and buttons. Both can be assembled quickly from parents and are highly intriguing to young children.

How do teachers decide how many items to start with?

This varies with the age of the class. Many of the collections described in this chapter were created for multi-age preschool classrooms. This is reflected in the number of pieces suggested for the starter sets. For very young classes, teachers may wish to reduce the number of items as well as the number of attributes. For kindergarten classes, the starter set might be larger.

What is the teacher's role?

The teacher must observe carefully, model appropriately, and direct her questioning to encourage a variety of sorting possibilities.

Teachers should allow ample time for the class to explore the materials in the collection and observe how children begin to group the items. They may discover a variety of sorting possibilities.

As interest wanes or the children appear to have exhausted all the possibilities, the teacher can model sorting by a new attribute or can ask questions to possibly lead their thinking in another direction:

▲ Is there another way to put these together?

▲ Do you have any that will fit in my group?

▲ Where can I put these?

▲ What would you do if you could only have four groups?

▲ How will (or did) you decide which ones go together?

When interacting with children, the teacher's goal should not be to provide solutions or present the "correct" way. Therefore, teachers should be prepared to back off quickly when questions do not stimulate new thinking. Otherwise, children may feel pressured and begin to avoid math materials.

What are some pitfalls to avoid?

▲ *Avoid "traditional" math materials such as shapes.* They are often less intriguing to children.

▲ *Do not try to force children to sort the collection based on your predetermined attributes.* The goal is to facilitate divergent and autonomous thinking.

Where can teachers get materials for collections?

▲ craft and fabric stores

▲ nature walks

▲ flea markets

▲ discount stores

▲ drug or hardware stores

▲ PARENTS

How should collections be displayed?

Collections should look attractive, be readily available to children, and be placed with containers that facilitate sorting. Collections are usually displayed in the manipulative area of the classroom where children can explore them for extended periods of time. Plan to leave a collection out for several weeks so that children can have ample time to explore, sort, and classify the items in many different ways. Additional collection pieces can gradually be added to encourage further sorting and to maintain interest.

Collections are often placed in an attractive basket along with a divided tray or smaller baskets to encourage sorting. Five or six sorting compartments are typical. See the individual collections in this book for more unusual display ideas.

How can teachers assess children's use of collections?

Teachers can monitor each child's use of the collections by writing anecdotal notes or recording their observations on either a class or an individual assessment sheet. All three methods enable teachers to chart each child's construction of logical-mathematical knowledge through sorting and classification in a natural setting. This, in turn, can guide teachers as they plan for both individual children and the entire class.

Some teachers monitor each child's progress in all areas through anecdotal notes kept either in a notebook with a section for each child, a portfolio for each child, or a file box. Notes about how each child used a collection can be included in this dated, running record.

Some teachers may prefer to use an assessment sheet to chart progress in a specific area. Two types of assessment forms for collections are included here. The class assessment form (figure 3.1) allows the teacher to list all of the children and check the attributes they sort by as they use a given collection. An advantage to this form is that the teacher can quickly note which children used a collection frequently and which children seldom or never did. This can guide the teacher in selecting future collections. (See A.3 in the appendix for a blank class assessment form for collections.)

The individual assessment form (figure 3.2) allows the teacher to chart an individual child's use of all the collections throughout the year. An advantage to this form is that developmental changes and a year-long progression are clearly evident. (See A.4 in the appendix for a blank individual assessment form for collections.)

Figure 3.1 Class Assessment Form for Collections

Collection: Hats   Date: 3/9/95

Name	Sorts by			
	color	type	size	material
Nancy	X	X		X
Mark	X	X		
Sanjay	X		X	

Figure 3.2 Individual Assessment Form for Collections

Child: Nancy

Collection	Sorts by, Date			
nuts	type 9/15	size 9/20		
clothespins	color 10/15	size 10/17	type 10/23	
keys	size 11/15	size 11/18		

Collection Activities

3.1 Keys

Materials

▲ an assortment of keys
▲ cup-hook frame on which to hang the keys, or hooks on the pegboard backing of shelves

Child's Level
older preschool or kindergarten

Possible Attributes
color—brass, silver, bronze
shiny or dull
shape
lines
printing
size of holes
shape of holes
number of holes

Starter Set
40 to 45
brass and silver
2 sizes

Helpful Hints

Children often want to take the keys around the room and try to open doors with them or use them in dramatic play. You might want to put some keys on a special ring and designate those for use in dramatic play.

Spray-paint some keys to create additional colors.

Ask parents to donate keys.

Ask hardware stores for defective keys they may otherwise discard.

What to Add
keys attached to rings
keys with more holes
red, blue, or green keys

What to Look For
Children often initially sort keys by color.
Children may sort by any of the listed attributes, or by attributes of their own invention.
Children may quantify types of keys.
Some children will compare how many keys are in each group.

Questions to Extend Thinking
Why did you put these keys together?
Where should I put this key?
Look! This key has lines. I wonder if any other keys have lines.

Integrated Curriculum Activities
Allow children to estimate the number of keys in a jar.
Use keys as counters for a grid game (see chapter 4).
Create opportunities for patterning with keys.

3.2 Buttons

Materials
- ▲ a variety of buttons
- ▲ sewing box for sorting
- ▲ 2 or 3 types

Child's Level
preschool or kindergarten

Possible Attributes
color
size
material—wood, metal,
   fabric, plastic, leather
shape
number of holes
design
metallic or nonmetallic

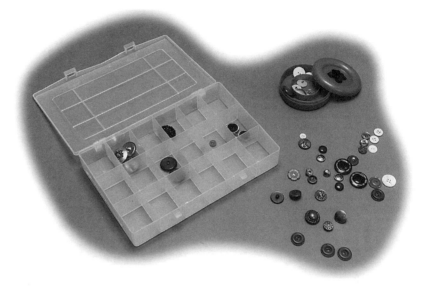

Starter Set
35 to 40
3 or 4 colors

What to Add
10 to 20 more buttons with the same colors but additional attributes—fabric, flower shapes, additional detail

What to Look For
Children usually focus on color when they initially sort buttons.
Children may sort by any of the listed attributes, or by attributes of their own invention.
Children may quantify types of buttons.
Some children may compare how many buttons are in each group.

Questions to Extend Thinking
How did you decide where to put the buttons?
Are there any buttons that will go into my pile?
Here are some new buttons. Where can they fit?

Integrated Curriculum Activities
Include the books *The Button Box* by Margarette S. Reid (Dutton Children's Books, 1990) and *Corduroy* by Don Freeman (Viking Press, 1968) in the reading area.
Collect buttons at the end of a short path game (activity 5.3), if appropriate for your group.

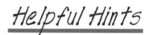

Helpful Hints

Buttons have so many attributes that a collection that is not carefully preplanned by the teacher can be overwhelming. Limit the number of attributes at first and gradually add more buttons with more attributes.

Avoid the smallest buttons with a young class of children who may still put things into their mouths.

3.3 Shoes

Idea by Carla Nordgren

Materials

- ▲ fashion doll shoes
- ▲ plastic shoes from ponytail holders
- ▲ small shoes and boots from craft and novelty stores
- ▲ divided tray

Child's Level

older preschool or kindergarten

Possible Attributes

color
type of shoes
size
design on shoe
flat or three-dimensional
material—plastic, leather, cloth

Starter Set

30 to 35
3 or 4 different types
2 or 3 colors

Helpful Hint

We found packets of fashion doll shoes and shoe ponytail holders at local dollar stores.

What to Add

larger size sneakers
cowboy boots
skates

What to Look For

Many children initially sort shoes by type.
Children may sort by any of the listed attributes, or by attributes of their own invention.
Children may quantify types of shoe.
Some children will compare how many shoes are in each group.

Questions to Extend Thinking

How did you decide where to put these shoes?
Where should these flat shoes go?
If a shoe is flat and also a cowboy boot, where should it go?
Which type of shoe do you have the most of?
Are there any shoes and boots that are the same color?
Where can these bigger shoes go?

Integrated Curriculum Activities

Include the books *I Went Walking* by Sue Williams (Harcourt Brace Jovanovich, 1989), *New Blue Shoes* by Eve Rice (Macmillan, 1975), and *Shoes* by Elizabeth Winthrop (Harper & Row, 1986) in the reading area.

Try shoe printing using key chain shoes or baby shoes and paint.

Make footprints by painting the children's feet and allowing them to walk down a strip of paper.

Set up a shoe store in the dramatic-play area.

Graph children's shoes (activity 6.3).

3.4 Hats

Material
▲ plastic hats from ponytail holders
▲ plastic toy hats
▲ straw, plastic, and felt caps and hats from craft stores
▲ sorting tray

Child's Level
preschool or kindergarten

Possible Attributes
color
size
material—plastic, felt, straw
type of hat

Starter Set
30 to 35
2 or 3 different colors
3 or 4 varieties of types

What to Add
additional types of hats; additional colors

What to Look For
Some children initially sort hats by color; others focus on the type of hat.
Children may sort by any of the listed attributes, or by attributes of their own invention.
Children may quantify types of hats.
Some children will compare how many hats are in each group.

Questions to Extend Thinking
Which hats should go together?
Is there a different group this hat could go with?
Which of these hats might go in your group?

Integrated Curriculum Activities
Include the books *Caps for Sale* by Esphyr Slobodkina (Addison-Wesley, 1968), *Aunt Flossie's Hats* by Elizabeth Fitzgerald Howard (Clarion Books, 1991), *Hats Hats Hats* by Ann Morris (Lothrop, Lee, & Shepard, 1989), and *Who Took the Farmer's Hat?* by Joan L. Nodset (Scholastic, 1963) in the reading area.
Set up a hat shop in the dramatic-play area.
Use small hats as collection pieces for a game (activity 5.4).
Graph children's hats, perhaps by color one day and by a different attribute on another day.

Helpful Hint

Avoid baseball and football hats with racially stereotypical logos.

3.5 Paper Clips

Materials
- ▲ assortment of plastic and metal paper clips
- ▲ small divided box or desk drawer divider

Child's Level
older preschool or kindergarten

Possible Attributes
color
shape
size
type of material
striped or solid color

Starter Set
45 to 50
3 colors
2 sizes

What to Add
additional colors, sizes, and shapes

What to Look For
Children usually focus on color when they initially sort paper
    clips.
Some children hook paper clips together. This allows the teacher
    to focus on quantification.
Children may create patterns with the clips.
Children may sort by any of the listed attributes, or by attributes
    of their own invention.
Children may quantify types of paper clips.
Some children will compare how many paper clips are in each
    group.

Questions to Extend Thinking
Where will you put these clips?
How do these clips go together?
Is there another kind of clip that could go with this one?

Integrated Curriculum Activity
Set up an office in the dramatic-play area.

Helpful Hint

Ask parents for paper
clips. You may receive
some unusual ones to
add to your collection.

3.6 Clothespins & Note Clips

Materials
▲ assortment of clothespins and note clips
▲ shelf extender rack to sort them onto (see photo), or box with clothesline strung across it

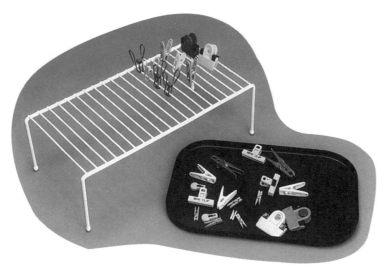

Child's Level
older preschool or kindergarten

Possible Attributes
size
material—plastic, metal, wood
color
type of clothespin—push or pinch
shape
magnetic back

Starter Set
30 to 35
2 colors
a variety of sizes, shapes, and materials

What to Add
additional colors (at least two more)
more wooden clothespins
larger display rack

Helpful Hints

Plan to allow extensive time for children to manipulate the clips. The fine motor skill is very intriguing.

Spray-paint wooden clothespins to correspond to plastic clothespin colors.

What to Look For
Children usually concentrate on clipping the clothespins onto the rack when they first use the collection.
Some children initially sort clothespins and note clips by color; others focus on type.
Children may sort by any of the listed attributes, or by attributes of their own invention.
Children may quantify types of clothespins.
Some children will compare how many clothespins are in each group.

Questions to Extend Thinking
Why are these clothespins together?
Which row has the most clothespins?
Is there a way to get all the metal clips onto one row?

Integrated Curriculum Activities

Include the book *The Wind Blew* by Pat Hutchins (Macmillan, 1974) in the reading area.

Wash doll clothes and hang them up to dry.

Dramatize the "Shirt" song from the recording *Make Believe in Movement* by Maya Doray (Kimbo Educational, 1976).

Add a drying rack and pretend washing machine to the dramatic-play area.

3.7 Bottle Caps & Lids

Materials
▲ assorted sizes, colors, and types of bottle caps and lids
▲ divided tray

Child's Level
preschool

Possible Attributes
color
size
type of lid—flip, pull up, screw on
words or not
ridges
material—plastic or metal
shape

Starter Set
35 to 40
3 colors
several sizes and shapes

What to Add
metallic bottle caps
additional colors
additional shapes

Helpful Hint

Bottle caps and lids are good items to have parents collect for you.

What to Look For
Children often initially sort bottle caps by color.
Children may sort by any of the listed attributes, or by attributes of their own invention.
Children may quantify types of bottle caps.
Some children will compare how many bottle caps are in each group.

Questions to Extend Thinking
Where else could this bottle cap go?
Is there another place to put these caps?
Which group has the most bottle caps?
Here are three baskets. Which bottle caps should go into each basket?

Integrated Curriculum Activities
Add small bottles, lids, and eyedroppers to water in the sensory table.
Nail bottle caps into wood.
Put a basket of colorful bottle caps on the art shelf for a collage.

3.8 Sea Shells

Materials
▲ sea shells in various sizes, shapes, and colors
▲ sorting tray or baskets

Child's Level
preschool or kindergarten

Possible Attributes
type of shell
size
color
ridges or smooth
spiral or flat
barnacles or other shells attached
stripes

Starter Set
35 to 40
3 colors
3 or 4 types

What to Add
additional types of shells
additional sizes

What to Look For
Children usually focus on the type of shell when they initially sort shells.
Children may sort by any of the listed attributes, or by attributes of their own invention.
Children may quantify types of shells.
Some children will compare how many shells are in each group.

Questions to Extend Thinking
How did you decide which shells to put together?
Is there another type of shell that could go with this one?
Look! This shell has ridges. Do any other kinds of shells have ridges?

Integrated Curriculum Activities
Include the books *Blue Sea* by Robert Kalan (Greenwillow Books, 1979) and *Something Queer on Vacation* by Elizabeth Levy (Delacorte Press, 1980) in the reading area.
Add fish nets and shells to water in the sensory table.
Rub large, serrated shells together for rhythm instruments.
Set up shell wind chimes in the music area.

Helpful Hints

Look for shells that fit multiple categories. For example, use scallop shells of several sizes and colors. Then look for other types of shells that fit the same size and color categories.

Shells are good items to have parents collect for you.

Collections of very small shells are not appropriate for children who put objects into their mouths.

3.9 Bells

Materials

▲ various sizes, colors, and types of bells, such as jingle bells, cow bells, liberty bells, India bells, strawberry-shaped bells
▲ sorting tray or baskets

Child's Level
preschool or kindergarten

Possible Attributes
color—gold, copper, brass, silver, red
size
type of bell

Starter Set
35 to 40
2 types
3 colors
3 sizes

What to Add
additional types of bells
additional sizes

Helpful Hints

Children will naturally want to listen to the bells. Try putting some bells out in the music area of the classroom or use them during group time before introducing the bell collection.

Collections of very small bells are not appropriate for children who put objects into their mouths.

What to Look For
Children initially like to play the bells.
Children often focus on the type of bell when they first use this collection.
Children may sort by any of the listed attributes, or by attributes of their own invention.
Children may quantify types of bells.
Some children will compare how many bells are in each group.
Children who are visually impaired may sort this collection by sound.

Questions to Extend Thinking
How did you decide to put these together?
Can you find some bells that sound the same?
Does the big jingle bell sound the same as the little jingle bell?
If we sorted the bells just by sound, which ones would you put together?

Integrated Curriculum Activities
Sing "Jingle Bells" with the children, and allow children to accompany the song with jingle bell instruments.
Put 2 or 3 sizes of the same type of bell in the music or science area so children can experiment with how size affects sound.

3.10 International Money

Materials
▲ assorted international coins and game tokens
▲ clear coin purses for sorting, or a divided box or tray

Child's Level
kindergarten

Possible Attributes
color—silver, brass, copper
size
faces
other pictures
numerals
edges
thickness
country of origin (older children)

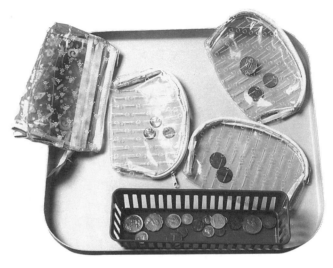

Starter Set
30 to 35
2 colors
3 sizes, some with faces

What to Add
additional coins with numerals
unique coins—scalloped edges, pictures, two-tone

What to Look For
Children usually focus on color when they initially sort coins.
Children may sort by any of the listed attributes, or by attributes
   of their own invention.
Children may quantify types of coins.
Some children will compare how many coins are in each group.

Questions to Extend Thinking
What type of coins should go into this purse?
Why do you think this coin with a "5" is bigger than this coin
   with a "10"?
Do all the coins have faces?

Integrated Curriculum Activities
Include the book *Alexander Who Used to Be Rich Last Sunday* by
   Judith Viorst (Atheneum, 1979) in the reading area.
Set up a grocery store in the dramatic-play area. Include only
   U.S. pennies so children can keep the money separate from the
   collection.

Helpful Hints

It is natural for young children to put coins into their pockets. You may want to remind the children at group time that the school money needs to stay in its own container.

Ask parents from other countries to donate coins.

Some banks may have international coins.

3.11 Jewels

Materials
▲ assorted jewels from craft and fabric stores, or clipped from flea market clothes
▲ treasure boxes for sorting

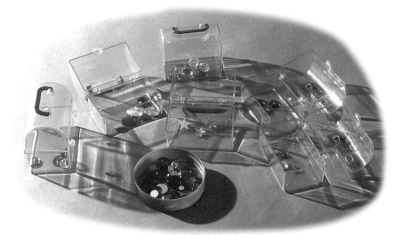

Child's Level
preschool or kindergarten

Possible Attributes
color
shape
size
iridescent quality
flat vs. faceted

Starter Set
55 to 60
3 colors
2 shapes
3 sizes

What to Add
flat jewels
combination jewels (such as buttons)
additional shapes

What to Look For
Children often initially sort jewels by color.
Children may sort by any of the listed attributes, or by attributes of their own invention.
Children may quantify types of jewels.
Some children will compare how many jewels are in each group.

Questions to Extend Thinking
Which jewels will you put together?
Is there another way to group them?
Here are some new jewels. Which group do these go with?
Do you have more red jewels or more blue jewels?
If we make three piles, how can we decide which jewels to put into each pile?

Helpful Hints

If you already have parents bringing in buttons, check to see if some are jeweled. This is a good way to augment your jewel collection.

This collection contains small pieces and is therefore not appropriate for children who put objects into their mouths.

Integrated Curriculum Activities

Include the book *Grandma's Jewelry Box* by Linda Milstein (Random House, 1992) in the reading area.

Add glitter or sequins to the art area.

Include the treasure path game (activity 5.20) as a math activity, if appropriate for your group.

 3.12 Bandages

Materials
▲ assorted bandages mounted on index cards and cut out
▲ divided first aid box for sorting

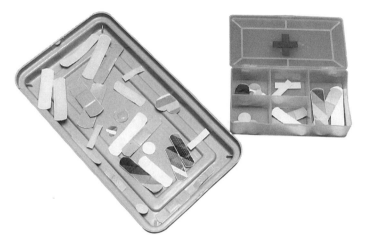

Child's Level
preschool or kindergarten

Possible Attributes
size
shape
color
plastic or fabric
design or pattern

Starter Set
35 to 40
3 colors
2 or 3 sizes of plastic bandages

What to Add
design bandages
different-shaped bandages
2 or 3 sizes of fabric bandages

What to Look For
Children usually focus on the type of bandage when they initially
  sort this collection.
Children may sort by any of the listed attributes, or by attributes
  of their own invention.
Children may quantify types of bandages.
Some children will compare how many bandages are in each group.

Questions to Extend Thinking
Where will you put these bandages?
Are there any other bandages for the little hurts? (This may help
  focus attention on size rather than color or shape.)

Integrated Curriculum Activities

Include the books *Betsy and the Doctor* by Gunilla Wolde (Random House, 1978), *Just Awful* by Alma Marshak Whitney (Addison-Wesley, 1971), and *Lotta's Bike* by Astrid Lindgren (R & S Books, 1989) in the reading area.

Include the doctor short path game (activity 5.1) and the bandage long path game (activity 5.13) as math activities, if appropriate for your group.

Set up a doctor's office in the dramatic-play area.

Helpful Hints

The colored bandages may come in only one size. You can cut these into smaller strips, circles, and hearts and thus get by with just one box.

Remove the peel-off backs from the bandages, mount them on an index card, and trim around them. If the children pull them off the cards, laminate them.

Children may want to bring a bandage from home to add to the collection.

3.13 Pom-Poms

Materials
▲ assorted pom-poms
▲ cans with pry-off lids (e.g., tea or chocolate drink cans)

Child's Level
preschool

Possible Attributes
color
size
glitter or not
material—fuzzy, spongy
homemade

Starter Set
45 to 50
3 colors
3 sizes
2 materials

What to Add
glitter pom-poms
homemade pom-poms

Helpful Hints

If children always sort by a particular attribute, such as color, reduce the amount of some colors so that they have to consider other ways to group the pom-poms.

The use of the cans with lids helps reduce the tossing of pom-poms that sometimes occurs when they are sorted into a tray or basket.

This collection contains small pieces and is therefore not appropriate for children who put things into their mouths.

What to Look For
Many children initially sort pom-poms by color.
Children may sort by any of the listed attributes, or by attributes of their own invention.
Children may quantify types of pom-poms.
Some children will compare how many pom-poms are in each group.

Questions to Extend Thinking
Is there another way to sort these pom-poms other than by color?
Where will you put the pom-poms with gold threads?
How many more pom-poms have gold threads?

Integrated Curriculum Activities
Put pom-poms and tongs in the sensory table.
Add yarn and cotton balls to the art shelf for a collage.
Use giant pom-poms as painting tools.

3.14 Rings

Materials

▲ assorted rings from craft and party stores, flea markets, and parent donations
▲ small jewelry box

Child's Level
preschool or kindergarten

Possible Attributes
color
material—metal, plastic, cloth, beads
jewels or not
design on band
size
clusters or not

Starter Set
40 to 50; 2 colors
2 types, jewels and plain

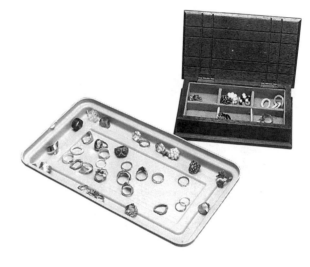

What to Add
additional bands with different shapes on the bands
clusters
additional colors

What to Look For
Expect children to initially want to try on the rings.
Some children initially focus on whether or not the rings have jewels.
Children often separate the rings they like from the rings they don't like.
Some children will put one ring onto each finger in one-to-one correspondence.

Questions to Extend Thinking
Which rings should go together in the jewelry box? Why?
Are there more rings with jewels or without jewels?
What if we didn't want all the gold rings together? How could we split them up?

Integrated Curriculum Activities
Include the book *Grandma's Jewelry Box* by Linda Milstein (Random House, 1992) in the reading area.
Set up a jewelry store in the dramatic-play area.
Include the treasure chest path game (activity 5.20) in the math area, if appropriate for your group.

Helpful Hints

Children like to wear the rings. You may want to put a particular type out in the dramatic-play area and designate those as the ones they can wear.

This collection contains small pieces and is therefore not appropriate for children who put objects into their mouths.

3.15 Nuts

Materials
▲ a variety of nuts
▲ divided tray or clear plastic jars
▲ tongs (optional)

Child's Level
preschool or kindergarten

Possible Attributes
color
size
shape
circle in center or not
texture
cap on or off (acorns)
smooth or rough
worm holes or not

Starter Set
30 to 35 nuts
3 varieties
2 sizes

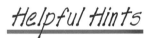

You may choose to avoid peanuts at first as children quickly crack these open.

Loose acorn caps can be glued onto the nut with a glue gun.

Collect tiny acorns or green acorns in late summer.

This collection contains small pieces and is therefore not appropriate for children who put objects into their mouths.

What to Add
2 to 4 additional varieties of nuts
additional details such as worm holes or caps

What to Look For
Children usually focus on the type of nut when they initially sort this collection.
Children may sort by any of the listed attributes, or by attributes of their own invention.
Children may quantify types of nuts.
Some children will compare how many nuts are in each group.

Questions to Extend Thinking
Which nuts go together?
Can this kind of nut fit with any other kind of nut?
Do any other kinds of nuts have a circle besides these?
If you closed your eyes and just felt the nuts, which ones would you put together?

Integrated Curriculum Activities

Take a nature walk to collect more nuts.

Allow children to estimate the number of buckeyes (or other large nut) in a clear jar.

Plan a nut tasting activity.

Include one of the long path games with nuts to collect (activities 5.12 and 5.18) as a math activity, if appropriate for your group.

3.16 Snowflakes

Materials
- ▲ snowflake spangles (from fabric stores)
- ▲ snowflakes cut from garlands
- ▲ sorting baskets or divided tray

Child's Level
preschool or kindergarten

Possible Attributes
color
size
formation
material—plastic, foil, wood,
  fabric
iridescent or non-iridescent

Starter Set
30 to 35
3 colors
2 sizes
2 types of material

What to Add
rounded snowflakes of all types
additional colors and materials

What to Look For
Children often focus on color when they initially sort the
  snowflakes.
Many children sort the snowflakes by size, or they may group
  "families" of snowflakes based on size and color (see anecdote
  3 in this chapter).
Children may sort by any of the listed attributes, or by attributes
  of their own invention.
Children may quantify types of snowflakes.
Some children will compare how many snowflakes are in each group.

Questions to Extend Thinking
Which snowflakes should go together?
Are there more red snowflakes or blue?
Are there more big snowflakes or small ones? (This may encour-
  age children to first group by size so they can answer the
  question.)

Integrated Curriculum Activities

Include winter books such as *The Snowman* by Raymond Briggs (Random House, 1978) and *The Snowy Day* by Ezra Jack Keats (Viking Press, 1962) in the reading area.

Dramatize snowflakes falling, blowing, swirling, and melting.

Make a class book. Children can dictate what they like to do in the snow and illustrate their pages.

Use snowflakes for counters on a grid game (activities 4.11 or 4.16).

Sing snow songs such as "It Was Snow," from *Discovering Music in Early Childhood* by Sally Moomaw (Allyn and Bacon, 1984— see B.3 in the appendix for the words and music).

Helpful Hints

Crocheted snowflakes make a wonderful addition to this collection. Perhaps you can find a parent or grandparent to crochet them.

You can cut snowflake shapes from cloth doilies and spray them with a commercial anti-fray compound available at fabric stores.

Snip off the ends of some snowflakes to create a rounded shape.

This collection contains small pieces and is therefore not appropriate for children who put objects into their mouths.

Interactions with Collections

ANECDOTE 1

Suzy (age 3½) was fascinated with the clothespin collection. She clipped all of the same type of clothespins together on the rack. Within these groupings, Suzy put clothespins of the same color together. Suzy repeated this activity for several days.

ANECDOTE 2

Jeffrey (age 5½) sorted a basket of tiny dinosaurs into groups of three. The teacher could observe no common attributes among the dinosaurs of each group. He asked Jeffrey how he decided which dinosaurs to put together. Jeffrey answered, "Well, I wanted three in each group, but I wanted each of the three to be totally different."

In this case the teacher could have erroneously assumed that the child could not sort the dinosaurs. His open-ended question elicited important information. Not only could the child classify, but he could mentally handle multiple attributes simultaneously in order to screen for his "totally different" set requirement. This showed a way of thinking the teacher had not anticipated for the child's age.

ANECDOTE 3

Reina (age 5) sorted a snowflake collection several times over a period of two weeks. She first grouped the snowflakes by color, but later she focused on size. Eventually Reina coordinated size, color, and quantity as she grouped the snowflakes. She placed the snowflakes in groupings of three. Each group had one large snowflake and two small snowflakes of the same color.

Grid Games

Can you ever remember playing a bingo-type game in which you eagerly anticipated the next call to see if you would fill a row? Maybe you planned your strategy so you could complete a row *and* a column with just one more call. Children playing grid games often plan in similar ways:

▲ Just two more and I will fill my board.

▲ If I roll a three, I will cover as many as you have!

▲ How many more do you have?

Such comments from children are evidence of the type of mathematical thinking that emerges while they play grid games.

Teachers' Questions

What are grid games?

Grid games are bingo-type cards (but without letters and numbers) used in combination with dice or spinners and intriguing counters. Children play grid games by rolling dice or spinning a spinner and placing a corresponding number of counters onto their boards. The grids may be designed in a variety of configurations in order to provide interest or an increase in difficulty. They often include stickers or drawings that relate to the game's counters. Usually a game consists of two grid boards so that two children can each have their own board but still play the game together. This encourages social interaction, which also furthers mathematical development (Kamii 1982, p. 41).

Why is it important to include grid games in the math curriculum?

Grid games provide opportunities for children to create mathematical relationships by using interesting manipulative counters to create, compare, and quantify sets. Children are often drawn to grid games because of the uniqueness of the manipulative counters, especially if they coordinate with satisfying literature, a field trip, or some other curricular event. As children interact with grid boards and counters, they are mentally active in the creation of mathematical relationships. They might wonder:

▲ How many do I take when I roll three dots on the die?

▲ How many more does my friend have than I do?

▲ Do we each have the same amount?

▲ How many fewer will I have if I give one to my friend?

Social-interaction and problem-solving situations also occur in the course of playing grid games:

▲ how to begin the game

▲ how to divide the counters

▲ what to do if two children want to play very different games using the same materials

▲ what to do if three people want to play

What makes a good grid game?

A good grid game has interesting counters and game boards with clearly delineated spaces to encourage one-to-one correspondence. The inclusion of a die or spinner encourages quantification.

What is wrong with commercial grid games?

There really are no commercial equivalents to the grid games introduced in this chapter. The closest commercial material is probably lotto games. Lotto games focus on matching picture cards to cards on a board and do not encourage the construction of mathematical concepts. Bingo games focus on letter and numeral matching rather than quantification.

What are the rules for grid games?

There are no specific rules. Instead, the children are encouraged to formulate their own rules for the games. This allows children to use the games at their own developmental levels.

Children often decide to use a die or spinner to determine how many counters to take. Even children who are too young to understand the relationship between dots on a die or spinner and a particular quantity of counters often use the die or spinner as part of their turn-taking routine. Teachers occasionally model using dice or spinners with children who have not yet progressed to that level. Teachers sometimes ask leading questions, such as "Can you take as many teddy bears as you rolled on the die?"

What math concepts emerge as children play grid games?

As children play with grid boards the concepts of one-to-one correspondence, comparison of sets, and addition emerge.

Grids are designed so that children are likely to perceive a one-to-one relationship between the counters and the spaces on the board. For example, a game with bunny stickers and carrot counters (activity 4.3) may encourage children to focus on placing one carrot counter onto each bunny sticker.

The process of rolling a die or using a spinner to determine the number of counters to take motivates children to attempt set comparisons. The games also give children the chance to observe other children who may be using different strategies. For example, some children use one-to-one correspondence to quantify as they point to a dot and then take a counter until all dots have been accounted for and all spaces on the grid filled. With amounts smaller than six, some children can *subitize* (perceive quantity without needing to count).

The concept of addition emerges when children begin to use two dice to play games. Many children combine the two dice by counting all the dots. Although the teacher should not expect to hear a child say, "Three plus one equals four," she may observe an understanding of addition when children combine the dots on a pair of dice or determine how many more are needed to fill the last spaces.

Other mathematical concepts may emerge naturally or in situations where the teacher poses questions such as those listed below:

SUBTRACTION

▲ How many more do you have than I do?

▲ How many will you have left if you put two back into the basket?

MULTIPLICATION

▲ Do you have enough so each space can have two? Are there enough for three on each space?

▲ How many more do we need so that we each have two on each space?

DIVISION

▲ How can we divide these so we each have the same amount?

What types of grid boards can teachers make?

One type of grid board consists of a small piece of poster board divided into individual blocks, with a sticker or illustration mounted within each space. (See, for example, activity 4.1, where silhouette stickers are mounted in the grid blocks.) This type of grid may attract children to the game because of the appealing stickers. Some children more easily create a one-to-one relationship between the counter and grid space when a sticker is in each space. The teacher can help children relate the math game to other aspects of the curriculum if the stickers correspond to those materials. For example, a grid with an autumn leaf sticker in each space may be coordinated with songs about the change of season. A grid with illustrations of babies (perhaps from wrapping paper) coordinates well with a doctor's office or new-baby thematic unit.

A second type of grid is marked into individual spaces but does not use stickers (see activity 4.4). These blank grids are versatile since they can employ a wide variety of counters, such as keys from the collection described in activity 3.1. Blank grids may not be attractive to children unless they have highly interesting counters. For example, children may approach a grid made with squirrel stickers and acorn caps (activity 4.5) with more enthusiasm than a blank grid with flat marble counters. The teacher should therefore use the most intriguing counters with blank grids.

A third type of board uses stickers to designate the spaces but is not marked into individual boxes (see activity 4.3). While such a game is appealing, some younger children may not perceive a one-to-one relationship between the counter and sticker with as much ease as with gridded boards. Teachers should observe children to determine the effectiveness of such grids in their particular groups.

What affects the difficulty of grid games?

The degree of difficulty is affected by the number of spaces on the grid, the number of dots on the die, and how many dice are used. Teachers should begin with games that are less complex in order to acquaint children with a new type of activity. Six- to ten-space grids and a 1-3 die or spinner make a good starting point. When materials or activities are too challenging, children sometimes misuse or avoid them. Since children will also ignore games that are too easy, teachers must be prepared to adjust the activities according to their observations of how children use them. Adding more spaces and counters, changing to a 1-6 die, or adding a second die all increase the difficulty.

What errors do children make when they play grid games?

Children make errors based on preoperational thinking. Most children go through a period where they use all the available counters. They continue to put counters onto the board even when each space is already covered. These children are not yet thinking about one-to-one relationships.

When children compare sets for equivalency, as when they spin a spinner and take counters, they frequently use perceptual cues for an extended period before quantifying more logically by one-to-one correspondence or by counting. Young children might make piles of objects or rows of counters that are the same length but are not the same quantity. Children who have progressed to the stage of counting may make counting errors such as skipping over or double-counting spaces and thus do not always quantify accurately.

What is the teacher's role?

Teachers plan inviting materials, observe, and model appropriately. They sparingly ask questions to encourage children to focus on higher-level concepts.

Children need ample opportunity to fully explore grid boards and counters. Many children are intrigued by the unique materials and may want to use them in a "pretend" fashion before focusing on the math game. Some children may not immediately create relationships between the manipulative counters and the grids. Therefore, after allowing a period of free exploration, the teacher may want to pose leading questions such as—

▲ What can you do with these game boards and counters?

▲ Do you have enough counters to put one on each space?

Later, after the teacher has repeatedly observed a child placing one object on each grid space, he can pose questions such as—

▲ Do you have enough to put two on each space?

▲ How many more do you need to put two on each space?

When children use dice with grid games, the teacher can observe which quantification strategies are employed. Some children roll the dice but do not think about a relationship between the dots and how many counters to take. When it is her turn the teacher can provide a model by describing what she does:

▲ I rolled a three—one, two, three (the teacher points to each dot as she counts)—so I'll take three counters, one, two, three.

What materials are needed for grid games?

Grid games are made from poster board and often use stickers or rubber-stamp designs. They are either laminated or covered with contact paper. Grid games also require interesting counters and dice. Poster board is readily available in a wide variety of appealing colors. Interesting counters may be found in toy stores, craft and fabric stores, large flea markets, catalogs, dollar stores, cake decorating shops, and yard sales. Teachers can begin by using items from their collections. Later they may find the perfect counters for a particular thematic unit, such as small carrot erasers to coordinate with *The Carrot Seed* by Ruth Krauss (activity 4.3). Look for counters such as—

▲ small wooden figures
▲ party favors
▲ cake decorations
▲ small erasers (one-inch)
▲ flattened glass marbles
▲ garlands to cut apart

What design problems should teachers consider when making grid games?

▲ Be sure the counters are sized to fit inside the marked spaces.
▲ The spaces should be arranged so that a counter does not cover more than one sticker or grid space.
▲ Avoid counters that can easily roll off of the grid board, such as nuts or vehicles with wheels.
▲ Use two sets of identical counters or two sets of equally appealing counters. This encourages children to discuss mathematical points of view rather than which counter is better. Younger children may need separate containers of counters for each player.
▲ Grid games will be more durable if they are laminated or covered with clear contact paper. Use watercolor markers for drawing lines when you plan to cover them with contact paper. Permanent markers will

"bleed" under contact paper and make the grids less attractive. Either type of marker can be used when the board is laminated.

▲ Evaluate the grids for attractiveness. Children will not be drawn to poorly made or unattractive materials. Stickers that are crooked or torn, illustrations that have been cut out in a jagged fashion, and lines that are smudged make grids less attractive.

▲ Design the grids to fit the surface you will use for display. If the game boards hang over the edge of the surface, such as a bench or table, children will inadvertently flip them off and spill the counters. This leads to frustration and sometimes general misuse of the game. Plan for two grids to fit together on the same surface so children can play side by side or across from each other. Children who must jockey for position cannot think about mathematical concepts!

How should grid games be displayed?

Grid games can be placed on a tray in the manipulative area or on a special game table. When grid games are placed on a tray together with all the game components, children can use them on the floor, either alone or with a partner. Grid games can also be displayed on a low bench or large hollow block, if there is room. This may be more inviting for some, since the games can be easily viewed by the children. A separate game table also provides a special place to highlight math activities and may attract to the area children who would not otherwise notice them. A small square table provides enough space for two players and is large enough to accommodate the largest grid boards without crowding. When grid games are the only type of board game in use, the game table is ideal for their display.

How can teachers use grid games as an assessment tool?

Teachers can observe children's thinking strategies, including uses of one-to-one correspondence, abilities to create equivalent sets, and development of counting principles. Natural settings are the most productive environments for children to explore materials and demonstrate their knowledge. Since grid boards are open-ended materials, they can be used in diverse ways depending on the levels of the children. They provide a risk-free setting in which children may try out ideas and solutions that they might avoid when directly asked questions in one-on-one assessment situations. Teachers can record anecdotal information in a note-book or on an assessment form. (See the assessment form examples in chapter 2 and the appendix.)

Note: For more information on natural settings, see *Developmentally Appropriate Practice in Early Childhood Programs Serving Children from Birth Through Age 8* (expanded edition) edited by Sue Bredekamp (NAEYC, 1988; p. 13); *Achievement Testing in the Early Grades* by Constance Kamii (NAEYC, 1990; p. 135), and *Transdisciplinary Play-Based Assessment* by Toni W. Linder (Paul H. Brookes Publishing, 1990; p. 15).

Grid Game Activities

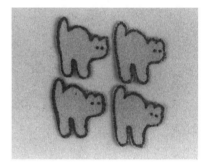

4.1 Silhouette Grid

Materials

▲ 2 grids, 4 by 12 inches, each with 6 stickers of children's silhouettes
▲ 12 tiny sunglasses (ponytail holders or erasers) to use as counters
▲ 1-3 spinner or die
▲ basket or container for counters

Child's Level

This is an appropriate introductory grid game for very young or inexperienced preschool children.

What to Look For

Children may use the spinner to determine how many sunglasses to take.

At first some children may play with the sunglasses without relating them to the game.

Children may place one pair of sunglasses onto each silhouette.

Children may compare how many sunglasses they each have.

Some children will count the sunglasses.

Modifications

After a short period of exploration, add more sunglasses so that each child has 12 pairs and can put two pairs on each sticker, if desired.

Add different types so that each child has, for example, 6 heart-shaped and 6 star-shaped sunglasses and can put one of each type on each sticker.

Use different counters such as hats, rings, or crayon erasers.

Older children can use the sunglasses on grids with more stickers. They can also use a 1-6 die or two dice.

Questions to Extend Thinking

Do you have enough sunglasses so that each child can have one pair?

Do you have as many red sunglasses as yellow ones?

How many more would you need to give each child two pairs?

Integrated Curriculum Activities

Provide sunglasses for outdoor activities.

Set up a beach in the dramatic-play area. Include sunglasses.

A spinner is easier to use than a die for some young children.

Be sure each child has the same type of sunglass counters for the initial experience. They will not focus on mathematical concepts if they argue about who gets the heart-shaped sunglasses versus the star-shaped ones.

Be sure to mark the poster board into individual sections.

4.2 Pinwheel Grid

Materials

- ▲ 2 grids, 8 by 6 inches, each with 8 pinwheel stickers
- ▲ 16 small wooden or plastic people
- ▲ small basket for counters
- ▲ 1-3 spinner or die

Child's Level

This game is most appropriate for children who are constructing one-to-one correspondence and are just beginning to quantify from one to three.

What to Look For

Children often spin the spinner, take a corresponding number of people, and place one per pinwheel sticker.

At first some children may play with the people without relating them to the game board.

Some children will place one person onto each pinwheel sticker without using the spinner. They are working on one-to-one correspondence.

Children may compare the number of people they each have.

Modification

Provide more people than available grid spaces so children will think about concepts other than one-to-one correspondence.

Questions to Extend Thinking

Are there enough pinwheels for each person to have one? How do you know?

Do you each have the same amount of people?

How many more people do you need so each pinwheel has one person?

Integrated Curriculum Activities

Include the books *It Looked Like Spilt Milk* by Charles G. Shaw (Harper & Row, 1993), *Titch* by Pat Hutchins (Macmillan, 1971), and *The Wind Blew* by Pat Hutchins (Macmillan, 1974) in the reading area.

Use pinwheels outside in the wind.

Set out pinwheels in the science area. Allow children to explore how to make them move.

Helpful Hints

Use dark poster board to make the grids.

Do not use people that are identical to others already on the manipulative shelves. Young children may remove them from the math game to add them to the manipulatives.

4.3 Rabbit Grid

Materials

▲ 2 grids, 7 by 5 inches, each with 12 rabbit stickers
▲ 24 carrot erasers
▲ 1-3 die
▲ 1 or 2 small containers for counters

Child's Level

This game is most appropriate for children who are constructing one-to-one correspondence or quantifying to three.

What to Look For

Children may roll the die to determine how many carrots to take and give one carrot to each rabbit.

A few children may roll the die and place an equivalent amount of carrots on one rabbit sticker.

Children may compare the quantities of carrots they each have.

Children may count the number of carrots each rabbit has.

Modifications

Add more carrots so that children can give each rabbit more than one carrot.

Change to a 1-4 or 1-6 die.

Put all the carrots into one basket to encourage the children to divide the materials before the game starts.

Helpful Hint

Use this game with children who will not chew the erasers.

Questions to Extend Thinking

Does each rabbit have the same amount of carrots?

How many more do you need so that each rabbit has the same number of carrots?

How many would there be if each rabbit ate one?

Integrated Curriculum Activities

Include the book *The Carrot Seed* by Ruth Krauss (Harper/Festival, 1973) in the reading area.

Make carrot raisin salad with the children.

Plant carrot seeds.

4.4 Vegetable Grid

Materials

- ▲ 2 grids, 6 by 6 inches, each marked into 9 sections
- ▲ 18 small wooden vegetables
- ▲ 1-3 die
- ▲ 2 small baskets for vegetable counters

Child's Level

This blank grid is most appropriate for children who are constructing one-to-one correspondence or quantifying to three.

What to Look For

Children may roll the die and take a corresponding amount of vegetables to place one per grid space.

Children may play with the vegetables and talk about likes and dislikes.

Some children may place one vegetable per grid space and not use the die. They are working on one-to-one correspondence.

Modification

To increase the difficulty, use a 12-space blank grid with more vegetable counters.

Questions to Extend Thinking

Do you have more than one of each vegetable?

How many more do you need to fill all the spaces?

If you could eat all the vegetables you like, how many would be left?

Do you have more green vegetables or more yellow ones?

Integrated Curriculum Activities

Include the books *Eating the Alphabet* by Lois Ehlert (Harcourt Brace Jovanovich, 1989) and *Growing Vegetable Soup* by Lois Ehlert (Harcourt Brace Jovanovich, 1987) in the reading area.

Make vegetable soup with the children. Each child can bring one vegetable from home.

Take a field trip to a local grocery store or market.

Wash vegetables in the sensory table or in tubs.

Create a grocery store in the dramatic-play area.

Have a "taste test" and graph the children's favorite vegetables.

Helpful Hints

Look for the wooden vegetable figures in craft stores or novelty catalogs.

Avoid using the counters in combination with a grid made of vegetable stickers. Children try to match the counters to the stickers and do not think about quantification.

4.5 Squirrel Grid

Materials

▲ 2 grids, 8 by 8 inches, each with 9 squirrel stickers
▲ 18 acorn caps
▲ 1-3 die
▲ 2 small baskets for the acorn cap counters

Child's Level

This grid is most appropriate for children who are constructing one-to-one correspondence or quantifying small amounts using a die.

What to Look For

Children may roll the die and take a corresponding number of acorn caps to place one per squirrel.

A few children may roll the die and place an equivalent amount of acorn caps on one squirrel sticker.

Some children may compare quantities of acorn caps.

Some children will count the acorn caps.

Modifications

Provide larger quantities of acorn caps so that children can place more than one per squirrel.

Change to a 1-4 or 1-6 die.

Questions to Extend Thinking

How many more acorn caps do you need to fill your grid?

If you want each squirrel to have two acorn caps, how many more will you need?

Do you each have the same amount?

Integrated Curriculum Activities

Include the book *Nuts to You!* by Lois Ehlert (Harcourt Brace Jovanovich, 1993) in the reading area.

Sing autumn and squirrel songs.

Include the nut collection (activity 3.15) in the manipulative area.

Select an autumn path game (activity 5.7, 5.12, or 5.18) that is appropriate for your group.

Put acorns, tongs, and baskets in the sensory table.

Crack open nuts with a block of wood as a science activity or for nut tasting.

Helpful Hint

Acorns roll off the grid easily and children become frustrated. This is why we suggest acorn caps for counters.

4.6 Leaf Grid 1

Materials

- ▲ 2 grids, 9 by 6 inches, each with 10 autumn leaf stickers
- ▲ 20 red marble chips, or 10 red and 10 yellow marble chips, so that each player has one color
- ▲ 1-3 spinner
- ▲ 2 baskets for the counters

Child's Level

This grid is most appropriate for children who are constructing one-to-one correspondence or quantification to three.

What to Look For

Children often use the spinner to decide how many counters to place on the leaf stickers.

Some children will place one marble chip per leaf sticker.

Some children will place one marble chip on each dot of the spinner!

Some children will count the dots on the spinner; some will use one-to-one correspondence to decide how many counters to take.

Modification

Try a 15-space grid board and a 1-6 die for children who are quantifying to six.

Questions to Extend Thinking

How do you know how many counters to take?

If you get three dots on your next turn, will you fill all the leaves?

Do we each have the same amount? How do you know?

Integrated Curriculum Activities

Include autumn books such as *Red Leaf, Yellow Leaf* by Lois Ehlert (Harcourt Brace Jovanovich, 1991) in the reading area.

Share autumn songs and poems with the children.

Make leaf rubbings.

Use black for the grids. The contrast to the autumn leaf stickers is attractive.

Look for realistic leaf stickers in nature stores or museum gift shops.

4.7 Teddy Bear Grid

Materials

▲ 2 grids, 10 by 5 inches, each with 10 rubber stamp pictures of the character, Corduroy

▲ 20 buttons in two colors

▲ 2 small baskets for counters

▲ 1-3 die

Rubber stamp pictures of Corduroy, copyright Don Freeman for Kidstamps, 1993

Child's Level

This grid is most appropriate for children who are constructing one-to-one correspondence or quantification to three.

What to Look For

Children may roll the die, take a corresponding amount of buttons, and place one per bear stamp.

Some children will place one button per bear stamp but not use the die. They are working on one-to-one correspondence.

Children may compare quantities of buttons they each have.

Some children will count buttons.

Some children may create patterns with buttons such as large/small, large/small or red/blue, red/blue.

Modifications

Change the type of buttons.

Change to a 1-6 die and provide more button counters. Perhaps the children will give each bear two buttons.

Questions to Extend Thinking

Do you each have the same amount of buttons?

Do you have enough to put two on each bear?

How can we divide the buttons so that each person has the same amount of each color?

Integrated Curriculum Activities

Include the books *Corduroy* by Don Freeman (Viking Press, 1968) and *The Button Box* by Margarette S. Reid (Dutton Children's Books, 1990) in the reading area.

Provide a button collection for sorting (activity 3.2).

Collect buttons at the end of a short path game (activity 5.3), if appropriate for your group.

Ask the children to bring a button from home. For kindergartners, estimate how many buttons will have four holes, two holes, and so on.

Younger children may mix the button collection (activity 3.2) in with the game buttons, so you might not want to put them out at the same time.

Use light brown or tan poster board so that the Corduroy picture looks like the book. You could color in the pants with green marker.

Use this game with children who no longer put things in their mouths.

4.8 Snowman Grid

Materials

▲ 2 grids, 12 by 6 inches, each with 12 snowman stickers
▲ 24 white pom-poms
▲ 1-3 die
▲ small basket for pom-poms

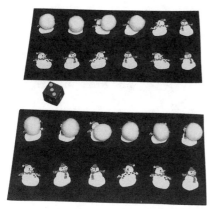

Child's Level

This grid is most appropriate for children who are experienced using 6- to 9-space grids and a 1-3 die.

What to Look For

Children may roll the die to determine how many pom-poms to take and place one per sticker.

Some children will ignore the die and use the pom-poms to build a snowman!

Children may compare quantities of pom-poms.

Modifications

Add more pom-poms so that children who are already secure with one-to-one correspondence can place more than one pom-pom per snowman.

Use plastic snowflakes from the snowflake collection (activity 3.16) in place of pom-poms.

Questions to Extend Thinking

Do you have enough pom-poms to put one on each snowman?

How many snowmen can you make if you use three pom-poms for each? (Use this question if the child uses the pom-poms to build snowmen.)

If two melt, how many will be left?

Integrated Curriculum Activities

Include winter books such as *The Snowy Day* by Ezra Jack Keats (Viking Press, 1962), *The Mitten* adapted by Jan Brett (G. P. Putnam's Sons, 1989), and *The Jacket I Wear in the Snow* by Shirley Neitzel (Greenwillow, 1989) in the reading area.

Sing winter songs such as "It Was Snow," from *Discovering Music in Early Childhood* by Sally Moomaw (Allyn and Bacon, 1984; see B.3 in the appendix for the words and music).

Provide a snowflake collection (activity 3.16) for sorting.

Select a winter path game (activity 5.10 or 5.21) that is appropriate for your group.

Helpful Hints

Do not substitute cotton balls for pom-poms since children easily tear cotton balls apart.

Use black or dark blue poster board for the grid.

4.9 Toothbrush Grid

Materials

- ▲ 2 grids, 12 by 5 inches, each with 10 drawings of toothbrushes
- ▲ 20 or more small plastic toothpaste tubes
- ▲ 1-3 or 1-4 die
- ▲ 1 or 2 containers for counters

Child's Level

This grid is most appropriate for children who are constructing one-to-one correspondence or quantifying to three or four.

What to Look For

Children often roll the die and take a corresponding number of tubes to place one per toothbrush.

A few children may roll the die and place an equivalent amount of tubes on one toothbrush drawing.

Children may compare how many of each brand they have.

Some children will disregard the die and place one tube of each brand onto each toothbrush. They are working on one-to-one correspondence.

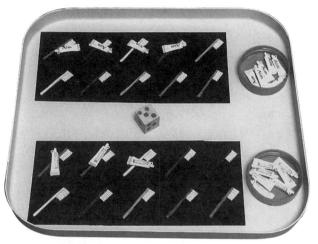

Drawings in the photo by Cindy Schneider

Modification

Add more tubes of toothpaste so that children will think of relationships other than one-to-one correspondence.

Questions to Extend Thinking

Do we each have the same amount of Crest toothpaste tubes? How many more do you need?

Do you have enough Aim toothpaste to put one on each toothbrush? How do you know how many more are needed?

Integrated Curriculum Activities

Include the book *My Dentist* by Harlow Rockwell (Greenwillow Books, 1975) in the reading area.

Sing the song "Brush Your Teeth" from *Singable Songs for the Very Young*, sung by Raffi with Ken Whiteley (Troubadour Records, 1976).

Paint with old toothbrushes.

Allow children to vote for their favorite toothpaste, and graph the results.

Helpful Hints

Look for the toothpaste tubes in novelty stores.

Use the toothpaste tubes with the silhouette grid (activity 4.1) if you have trouble drawing toothbrushes.

Use people figures if toothpaste tubes are not available.

4.10 Letter Grid

Materials
▲ 2 grids, 9 by 9 inches, each with 16 stickers of envelopes, post cards, and writing paper
▲ 32 small wooden or plastic people
▲ 1-6 die
▲ basket for counters

Child's Level
This game is most appropriate for children who are ready to quantify to six and use larger quantities of counters.

What to Look For
Children often roll the die and take a corresponding number of people to place one per letter. Some children will place one person per letter without using the die. They are working on one-to-one correspondence.
At first some children will play with the people and not think about the math.
Some children will count or compare the number of people they each have.

Helpful Hints

Use marble chips as counters if you do not have small people.

Do not use marble chips with children who will put them into their mouths.

Modification
Use crayon erasers or ponytail holders for counters.

Questions to Extend Thinking
How many more people do you need to cover all the letters?
Do we each have the same amount of letters left to cover?
If you cover two more, will you cover all the letters on the grid?

Integrated Curriculum Activities
Include the books *A Letter to Amy* by Ezra Jack Keats (Harper & Row, 1968) and *The Jolly Postman* by Janet and Allan Ahlberg (Little, Brown, 1986) in the reading area.
Select a letter path game (activity 5.6 or 5.16) that is appropriate for your group.
Set up a post office in the dramatic-play area.
Include envelopes and stamps in the writing area. Use stamps from book or record club mail-order promotions.

4.11 Snowflake Grid 1

Materials
- ▲ 2 grids, 8 by 8 inches, each with 16 snowflake stickers
- ▲ 32 snowman erasers, 16 with red hats and 16 with green hats
- ▲ 1-6 die
- ▲ 2 small baskets for the counters

Child's Level
This grid is most appropriate for children working on quantification to six.

What to Look For
Children often roll the die and take a corresponding number of erasers to place one per snowflake.

Some children will count the snowmen, and some children will compare the number of snowmen with red hats versus green hats.

Some children may create patterns on the grid such as green/red, green/red.

Modification
Add a red-green color die so more advanced children can think about two attributes—number of snowmen and color of hat.

Questions to Extend Thinking
Do you have just as many snowmen with red hats as green hats?
How many more snowmen with red hats do you need?
If you roll a four, will you be able to fill a row?

Integrated Curriculum Activities
Include winter books such as *The Snowy Day* by Ezra Jack Keats (Viking Press, 1962) and *The Snowman* by Raymond Briggs (Random House, 1978) in the reading area.
Select a path game with a snow or winter theme (activity 5.10 or 5.21), if appropriate for your group.
Spray-paint snow with colored water.

Helpful Hint
Use snowflakes from the snowflake collection (activity 3.16) if you cannot find snowman erasers.

4.12 Jewels for a Crown

Materials
▲ 2 grids, 12 by 9 inches, each with 16 tiny crown cutouts in several colors
▲ 32 colored marble chips as "jewels"
▲ 1-6 die
▲ jewelry box, treasure chest, or baskets to store "jewels"

Child's Level
This grid is most appropriate for children working on quantification to six.

What to Look For
Children may roll the die and take a corresponding amount of jewels.
Children may place one or more jewels onto each crown.
Some children will count to decide how many jewels to take; others will use one-to-one correspondence.
Some children will group the jewels by color and compare the quantities.
Some children will place jewels on crowns of the same color as the jewel.

Modifications
Change jewels from one color to several colors per player.
Provide more jewels so that children can place more than one jewel per crown.

Questions to Extend Thinking
How many more jewels will you need to have two for each crown?
Do you have just as many red jewels as green jewels?
How can we divide these so we have the same amount of each color?
Can we divide these into three equal groups?

Integrated Curriculum Activities
Include the books *King Bidgood's in the Bathtub* by Audrey Wood (Harcourt Brace Jovanovich, 1985) and *Grandma's Jewelry Box* by Linda Milstein (Random House, 1992) in the reading area.
Allow children to vote for their favorite character from *King Bidgood's in the Bathtub*. Graph the results (activity 6.8).
Set up a jewelry store in the dramatic-play area.

Helpful Hints

Use metallic paper for the crowns and gold or silver paint markers to draw grid lines.

Avoid using small jewels with children who put things into their mouths.

4.13 Leaf Grid 2

Materials

- ▲ 2 grids, 11 by 12 inches, each with 21 stickers of autumn leaves arranged in rows of 1, 2, 3, 4, 5, and 6 stickers
- ▲ 42 tiny squirrels
- ▲ 1-6 die
- ▲ 2 baskets for counters

Child's Level

This grid is most appropriate for children working on quantification to six or comparing sets from one to six.

What to Look For

Children may roll the die and take an equivalent quantity of squirrels to place one per leaf. They will begin with the row of one leaf and progress to the subsequent rows. For example, when the child rolls six dots, he covers the row with one leaf, then both spaces in the two-leaf row, then all three spaces of the three-leaf row.

Some children will roll the die and cover all the leaves in the row representing that quantity on the die. For example, when a child rolls six dots, she covers all the leaves in the six-leaf row.

Modification

Use acorn caps, walnuts, or other autumn seeds and pods as the counters.

Questions to Extend Thinking

Which leaves will you cover if you roll a five?
What will you do if all the leaves in the "two" row are covered and you roll another two?
Which rows can you fill if you roll a five?

Integrated Curriculum Activities

Include autumn books such as *Nuts to You!* (1993) and *Red Leaf, Yellow Leaf* (1991), both by Lois Ehlert (Harcourt Brace Jovanovich) in the reading area.
Share squirrel and autumn songs or poems with your class.
Create a nut collection (activity 3.15).
Put nuts, tongs, and clear plastic jars in the sensory table.
Provide nuts and leaves for collage material.
Take a nature walk.

Helpful Hints

Look for leaf stickers in nature stores and museum gift shops.

Use autumn colors for the grids.

Avoid using nuts that will roll off the grid.

4.14 Palm Tree Grid

Predictable Book
This game was designed to correlate with *Chicka Chicka Boom Boom* by Bill Martin, Jr., and John Archambault (Simon & Schuster, 1989), a predictable book where alphabet letters climb a coconut tree.

Materials
▲ 2 grids, 12 by 4 inches, each with 6 palm tree stickers
▲ 2 sets of small alphabet letters
▲ 1-4 die
▲ 2 baskets or coconut half-shells to display alphabet letters

Child's Level
Although this grid has only six spaces, it is intended for more advanced children. The large quantity of counters (26 letters) is overwhelming for less experienced children.

What to Look For
Children may roll the die and place a corresponding number of letters onto a palm tree sticker.
Some children may use the alphabet to spell words or simply talk about letters.

Modifications
Provide more alphabet letters.
Use a 1-6 die.

Questions to Extend Thinking
How can you divide the alphabet among the six palm trees?
Do you have just as many letters as I do?
Do you have enough letters to put three onto each palm tree? Are there enough for four per tree?

Integrated Curriculum Activities
Include the book *Chicka Chicka Boom Boom* in the reading area.
Include the palm tree game (activity 2.9) in the manipulative area.
Use coconut shells as tone blocks.
Use coconut shells as scoops in sand or water.
Put a variety of coconuts in the science area.

4.15 Chicken Grid

Predictable Book
This game is designed to coordinate with *Rosie's Walk* by Pat Hutchins (Macmillan, 1986).

Materials
- ▲ 2 grids, 8 by 5 inches, each with 12 rubber stamp pictures of Rosie the hen
- ▲ 48 or more kernels of feed corn
- ▲ 1-3 or 1-6 spinner made with corn
- ▲ basket to hold corn

Child's Level
This game is most appropriate for children who can quantify to six and may be interested in dividing the corn. The large amount of counters is intriguing to older, more experienced children. They can give each chicken more than one kernel of corn.

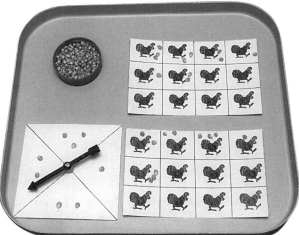

Rubber stamp pictures of Rosie the hen, copyright Pat Hutchins for Kidstamps, 1993

What to Look For
Children often roll the die and take a corresponding quantity of corn.
Some children will divide the corn evenly on the grid.
Children may count the corn and compare the quantities they have.

Modification
Use a pair of dice instead of the spinner for children who are ready for addition.

Questions to Extend Thinking
If each hen eats one kernel of corn, how many will be left?
Do you have enough corn for each hen to have the same amount? How will you find out?

Integrated Curriculum Activities
Include the book *Rosie's Walk* in the reading area.
Make prints with corn cobs and paint.
Put corn and farm animals in the sensory table.
Add farm animals to the block area.

Helpful Hints

Reduce the amount of corn available for younger children, since they may be more interested in dumping the corn than in quantifying it.

Use white poster board for the grid and use colored markers to fill in some details of the rubber stamp pictures.

4.16 Snowflake Grid 2

Materials
- ▲ 2 grids, 4 by 18 inches, each with 9 spaces
- ▲ 36 plastic snowflakes in two or more types, sizes, or colors
- ▲ 1-6 die
- ▲ container for counters

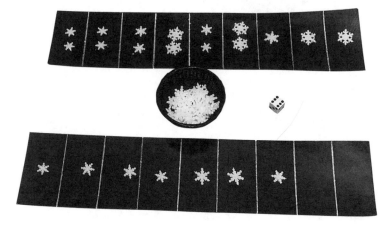

Child's Level
This grid is most appropriate for children who can quantify from one to six and can share one group of counters. These materials provide opportunities for patterning and repeated addition.

What to Look For
Children often roll the die and take a corresponding quantity of counters to place one per snowflake.

Some children will put two types of snowflakes on each sticker.
Some children may create a pattern such as large/small, large/small.

Modifications
Add a 1-3 die so that children who are ready for addition can combine it with the 1-6 die.
For kindergarten children, add a card that describes how many of each type of snowflake to place on the grid.

Questions to Extend Thinking
Do you have just as many large snowflakes as small ones?
Do you have enough to put three snowflakes onto each space?

Integrated Curriculum Activities
Include winter books such as *The Snowy Day* by Ezra Jack Keats (Viking Press, 1962) in the reading area.
Sing winter songs such as "It Was Snow," from *Discovering Music in Early Childhood* by Sally Moomaw (Allyn and Bacon, 1984; see B.3 in the appendix for the words and music).
Provide a snowflake collection (activity 3.16) for sorting.
Select a winter path game (activity 5.10 or 5.21) that is appropriate for your group.

Helpful Hints

Look for garlands of snowflakes at craft stores. Cut them apart to make counters.

Use black poster board for the grids. Use a white paint marker for grid lines.

4.17 Baby Grid

Materials
▲ 2 grids, 12 by 11 inches, each with 15 illustrations of babies
▲ 30 counters each of diaper pins, rattles, and pacifiers
▲ one or two 1-6 dice
▲ 3 small containers to store the counters

Child's Level
This grid is most appropriate for children who are quantifying to six or adding two dice together.

What to Look For
Children often roll the die and take a corresponding amount of one type of counter to place one per grid space.

Some children will try to collect one of each type of counter for each baby.

Some children will add two dice together by counting all the dots.

Some children will roll two dice but quantify them separately.

Modifications
For kindergarten children, add a card that lists the number of each type of counter to collect, for example, 10 rattles, 8 diaper pins, 7 pacifiers.

Use fewer counters for younger children.

Questions to Extend Thinking
Do you have just as many pacifiers as rattles? How do you know?
Do you have enough pacifiers to give each baby two?
How do you decide how many of each to take?

Integrated Curriculum Activities
Include the books *Before I Was Born* by Harriet Ziefert (Knopf, 1989), *Betsy's Baby Brother* by Gunilla Wolde (Random House, 1975), and *"More More More," Said the Baby* by Vera B. Williams (Greenwillow Books, 1990) in the reading area.
Sing the traditional song, "Hush Little Baby."
Set up a baby nursery in the dramatic-play area.
Wash dolls in the water table or tubs.
Have a parent and baby visit. Perhaps the parent can bathe the baby.

Helpful Hints

Begin with just thirty of one type of counter and later add other types of counters.

Be sure the illustrations represent a diverse population.

Magazines, greeting cards, and wrapping paper are good sources of pictures for the grid.

Baby item counters are interesting enough to use on a blank grid board.

4.18 Balloons

Materials

- ▲ 2 grids, 9 by 6 inches, each with 15 balloon stickers, with several stickers cut apart and "Pop!" written in the cut out space
- ▲ 30 small wooden or plastic people
- ▲ 1-6 die
- ▲ container to store people

Child's Level

This grid is most appropriate for children working on quantification to six. The popped balloons add a new dimension that encourages children to generate additional rules.

Helpful Hints

Do not use the small people at the same time that similar people are available in another classroom area. Younger children may mix the groups together.

Substitute marble chips if you do not have thirty small people and if the children will not put them into their mouths.

What to Look For

Children often roll the die and take a corresponding number of people to place one per balloon.

Some children will place one person on each balloon without using the die. They are working on one-to-one correspondence.

Some children may play with the small people in a dramatic-play manner.

Some children will compare the numbers of people they each have.

Some children may generate rules for the "Pop!" spaces such as, "those spaces are covered last" or "those spaces can't be covered."

Modification

Use two dice and additional counters (perhaps marble chips) for more advanced children.

Questions to Extend Thinking

Do you have enough people to give each one a balloon?

If you roll a four will you be able to use all the people left in the basket?

How many more people do you need to give each one a balloon?

Integrated Curriculum Activities

Include party books such as *Happy Birthday Sam* by Pat Hutchins (Viking Penguin, 1981), *Mary Wore Her Red Dress* by Merle Peek (Clarion Books, 1985), *My Presents* by Rod Campbell (Macmillan, 1989), and *A Letter to Amy* by Ezra Jack Keats (Harper Row, 1968) in the reading area.

Select a balloon path game (activity 5.4 or 5.23) that is appropriate for your group.

Use balloons for a gross-motor or creative-movement activity.

4.19 Dot Grid

Materials

▲ 2 grids, 12 by 7 inches, each with dots in sets from 1 to 6
▲ 21 small watering can counters
▲ 1-6 die
▲ small basket for counters

Child's Level

This grid is most appropriate for children who have had many experiences with grids and are interested in creating sets of objects from one to six. The dots may not be as appealing to younger children.

What to Look For

Children often roll the die and take a corresponding number of watering cans to place one per dot.

Some children may roll the die, take a corresponding number of counters, and find an equivalent set of dots to cover on the grid.

Modification

Substitute polished stones, shells, or other small counters.

Questions to Extend Thinking

What will you need to roll to fill this set? (Teacher points to a set of dots.)
How many more watering cans do you need to fill all the dots in this set?
If you roll a four, which dots will you cover?

Integrated Curriculum Activities

Include planting books such as *The Carrot Seed* by Ruth Kraus (Harper/Festival, 1973) and *Flower Garden* by Eve Bunting (Harcourt Brace, 1994) in the reading area.
Plant seeds and measure them as they grow.
Put watering cans in the sensory table.
Plan a seed collage as an art activity.
Set up a flower shop in the dramatic-play area.
Select a planting path game (activity 5.8 or 5.19) that is appropriate for your group.

Interactions with Grid Games

ANECDOTE 1

Bobby (age 3½) sat at the game table with the teacher to play a 12-space leaf grid game with a 1-3 spinner. They each had a basket of acorns to use as counters. The baskets originally contained twelve acorns each, but some of the acorns had become misplaced so that Bobby's basket had fifteen, while the teacher's had nine.

Bobby ignored the numbers he spun and instead placed one acorn on one leaf of the grid at each turn. When his grid was filled he had three acorns left in the basket, which he then dumped into the teacher's basket. The teacher then asked Bobby if they each had the same amount of acorns on their boards. As Bobby counted each group, he double-counted and skipped over some. He counted ten for his twelve acorns. He also counted the teacher's seven acorns on her grid as ten and ignored the acorns left in her basket.

Bobby had stable-order counting to ten, but not to twelve. Although he had some understanding of the phrase "same amount," since he attempted in his counting to make both sets have the same number of members, mathematically he was not able to compare the sets. Note that although Bobby does not use the principle of one-to-one correspondence in his counting, he nevertheless chose counting as his method for quantification.

ANECDOTE 2

Megan (age 5½) played a grid game that consisted of a 24-space board with basket stickers and a pair of 1-6 dice. The 24 counters were small flower erasers in three different colors. She rolled the dice and took a corresponding number of flowers. Megan placed one flower on each basket until all the stickers were covered and then placed a second flower onto each basket until each had two flowers. She stopped and rearranged the flowers in an attempt to have one red and one blue flower on each basket. When she did not have enough reds and blues, Megan bargained with her partner to trade all her yellow flowers for red and blue ones. Her partner agreed, and Megan continued placing flowers until each basket had a red and blue flower. When asked if she had just as many red as blue flowers, Megan said "yes" and spontaneously counted all the reds (12) and all the blues (13). She recounted both sets and this time counted 12 red and 12 blue. Megan exclaimed, "I knew they had to be the same because each basket has one blue and one red."

ANECDOTE 3

Jan (age 4) played a grid and counter game with a 1-6 die. When she rolled one, two, or three, she counted the dots and took the same number of counters. When she rolled four, five, or six, she turned the die back to one, two, or three. The teacher suspected that Jan was not yet comfortable with quantities higher than three.

Path Games

- ▲ Hurry! You need to roll at least a three to get past the cave.

- ▲ Let's say we get to move ahead one space every time we land on a gold star.

- ▲ If you give me two of your jewels, I can have three jewels on each crown.

- ▲ You don't have to count all of the dots. See, you just say "three" and then count these: 4, 5, 6, 7, 8.

Children often make these types of comments as they play teacher-developed path games. Their excitement, thinking, and peer interactions are evident. In order to resolve problems presented by the games, children often use mathematical strategies that are more complex than would be required by workbooks or many commercial math games. They get immediate feedback when they try to prove a point or when a peer disagrees. Since children are encouraged to be autonomous, they can alter the rules of the games as long as all the players agree. They can also increase the difficulty of the games or play the games in new ways that are individually appropriate for them.

Teachers' Questions

What are path games?

In path games, children roll dice to advance a mover along a path made of clearly defined spaces. Path games encourage social interaction as children engage in mathematical thinking and problem solving. Teachers can design the games to coordinate with topics of interest, field trips, or books in the classroom.

Why is it important to include path games in the math curriculum?

Path games incorporate the thinking strategies needed for grid games (see chapter 4) at a more difficult level and place additional emphasis on social interactions with teachers and peers. Moving along a path is more abstract than taking counters; therefore, path games are cognitively more difficult than grid games. Path games provide opportunities for children to discuss their ideas with others and be confronted with different opinions. When children defend their beliefs, they may strengthen their knowledge base or be forced to rethink how they view a situation. For example, when one child moves one space for each dot shown on the dice while the other child moves randomly, or when one child re-counts the space his mover is on and the other child does not, one or both of them may be bothered by the results. Over a period of time these interactions help children move toward more logical thinking.

What makes a good path game?

A good path game has a clearly defined path and intriguing movers that encourage children to move in one-to-one correspondence. It involves a topic that is interesting to children and often coordinates with other aspects of the curriculum. Good path games are attractive and durable.

What is wrong with commercial path games?

Commercial games generally do not encourage children to construct mathematical relationships or use their own thinking strategies. They are often too difficult or too easy. Some games, such as Chutes and Ladders, incorporate a long (100-space) and confusing path with a relatively simple 1-6 spinner. Games such as Candyland encourage children to use color matching rather than quantification strategies. (It is likely that these games were never intended to be mathematical materials.) Teachers may be unable to coordinate commercial games with other curriculum areas. Also, commercial math games do not provide opportunities for teachers to assess or plan for individual children.

What are the rules for path games?

There are no specific rules for path games. Children are encouraged to decide among themselves what the rules will be so that they can adapt the games to correspond to their own developmental levels. Children who are not being evaluated prefer more challenging material (see "Your Praise Can Smother Learning" by David L. Martin in *Learning*, Feb. 1977, p. 44). Therefore teachers need not worry that children will consistently play games below their cognitive level. In fact, children often create more difficult problems than teachers would ever think to give them. For example, a four-year-old child decided to double every roll of the dice and consistently did this throughout a game.

Children usually want to roll dice in order to tell how many spaces to move when playing path games. This seems to be a standard convention.

By kindergarten most children elect to play games competitively. They enjoy playing to win. This seems to be a natural part of development and occurs even in classrooms where teachers de-emphasize competition. As children get older, the excitement and fun of competition motivates them to play path games again and again.

What concepts emerge when children play path games?

As children interact with each other while playing path games, they continue to consider one-to-one correspondence, equivalence of sets, and addition, but at a more complex level.

Path games require children to think about one-to-one correspondence in a new context. Rather than take one counter for each dot on the dice, they must move one space along the path for each dot. This is more abstract because children cannot see a specific quantity of items to correspond to the number of dots on the dice.

When children construct equivalent sets in path games, the sets they must compare (the number of dots on the dice versus the number of spaces moved) are not as concrete as when they roll dice and take counters. They have to construct the idea that they can quantify spaces on the path before they can consider comparing a set of spaces to a number rolled on a die. This is why children can successfully play grid games before they are able to play path games, and why short path games are introduced before long path games.

Long path games are an ideal format for encouraging the addition of two dice, since the games have many spaces and children are eager to get to the end! Kindergarten children enjoy path games so much that many learn all the addition combinations just by playing the games.

What kinds of path games can teachers make and what affects their level of difficulty?

Teachers can make short path, long path, continuous path, and collection games. The level of difficulty of path games is affected by whether there are separate paths for each player or just one path for all players and by the length of the path. The number of dots on the die (1-3 versus 1-6), the number of dice used, and the addition of traps or collection spaces also affects the difficulty. Since the types of games vary in difficulty, teachers can select a specific type of path game to best approximate the cognitive level of specific children in the class.

Short path games are designed to help children transition from grid games to longer path games. Two identical paths are provided so that two children can parallel play. The two paths may be opposite each other on one game board or on separate game boards for younger children who have trouble sharing a single board. The paths should be straight and clearly delineated to avoid the perceptual confusion that curves sometimes cause. The paths generally consist of 10 to 12 spaces each, since more than twelve spaces can be overwhelming, while fewer spaces look like a grid rather than a path. A 1-3 die or spinner is used to determine the number of spaces to move, since a 1-6 die may be too challenging for children in this transition stage. In addition, a 1-6 die could end the game in only two rolls!

Long path games are used when children are ready for more challenging games. They contain 25 to 50 spaces along a curved path and may involve a variety of traps and bonus spaces that require the player to roll again, go back one space, or follow more original directions that the children themselves design. One or two 1-6 dice are used since children who can play long path games can usually quantify to six and may be ready to start adding two dice together.

Continuous path games do not have a definite start and finish point. The path has 25 to 50 spaces and is usually shaped in a square, oval, or circle. One or two 1-6 dice are used.

Collection games are variations of short path, long path, and continuous path games. Collection pieces on short path games encourage children to play them for a longer period of time. When collection pieces are used on a short path game, a shorter path may be desirable. Long path collection games may include special spaces where children stop and collect counters, or children may collect counters at the end of the path. Players may compare each other's quantities of items they have collected, or they may record their quantities on a piece of paper or on a graph. Long or continuous path collection games can provide an additional challenge for kindergarten children.

What errors do children make when playing path games?

Children make counting errors such as skipping over objects or double-counting as well as addition errors. Counting errors often continue for an extended period. However, when children make errors they are often corrected by their peers. Children who are challenged in their thinking by other children are forced to rethink their logic and ultimately move ahead in their thinking and stop making errors.

Another common error that children make is to re-count the space their mover occupies when they begin a new turn. Some children stop making this error after playing gross-motor path games (see activity 7.3) where they themselves are the mover.

Children who successfully use grid games often need a period of exploration with path games before they are able to play them in a conventional manner. Initially, some children roll the dice and hop along the path without regard to the quantity on the dice. They do not yet perceive the relationship between the roll of the dice and the spaces on the path. For some children the total length of a long path may be overwhelming. They may respond by moving from start to finish quickly.

What is the teacher's role?

The teacher plans developmentally appropriate games, encourages social interaction, and stimulates higher-level thinking strategies through questioning techniques or appropriate modeling.

Teachers must provide a variety of levels of games in order to best meet the developmental needs of an entire class. Grid games, short path, and long path games may all be appropriate for certain children. Teachers might want to create games on these three levels that all center around a common topic, such as autumn. Then, any child in the class who wanted to play an autumn game could find one on her level (activities 5.7, 5.12, and 5.18). This does not mean that the teacher should suggest that a child not play a particular game. Rather, the teacher should allow the children to play the game *in their own way* and perhaps afterward suggest another game that might be more appropriate.

Path games, especially long path games, require more social interaction among the participants than grid games, which are sometimes used by children in parallel-play fashion. The teacher should observe and facilitate these interactions but not offer solutions. The teacher maintains the role of a mediator to help children see each other's viewpoints and further their thinking. Younger children often seek the teacher as a partner for playing path games. They seem to enjoy a close relationship with the teacher. Most kindergarten children prefer peer interactions, but they may need the teacher to help mediate disputes or assist in problem solving.

The teacher can model alternative thinking strategies when it is her turn to play. For example, if a child has been adding two dice together by counting all the dots for an extended period, the teacher can model "adding on." After rolling a five and a three, the teacher, touching the five die, then touching each dot on the three die, might say, "I rolled a five; six, seven, eight." When the teacher models, she should not appear to indicate that the child's approach is incorrect. The teacher can model some social conventions of game playing for younger children, such as using the dice to determine how far to move, turn taking, and the meaning of traps and bonus spaces.

What materials are needed for path games?

Path games require poster board, stickers or rubber stamps, dice, and individual movers. These are essentially the same materials described for grid games. Unlike grid games, where the counters for each child are similar, path games should provide identifiable movers for each player. If the movers are identical, children cannot remember which mover is theirs. Children are drawn to path games because of the interesting board and movers. Look for movers such as the following:

▲ commercial plastic or wooden people, especially those that exhibit cultural diversity

▲ erasers

▲ party favors

▲ magnets

▲ wooden or resin figures

▲ cake decorations

What design criteria should teachers consider?

Teachers must carefully plan the path design, choose the movers, and select the type and number of dice. They should give attention to the aesthetic qualities of the game and consider the following issues:

▲ The topic should be interesting to children so they are motivated to play the game. It might coordinate with another aspect of the curriculum such as a book, field trip, or a thematic topic.

▲ The length and configuration of the path, including any traps or bonus spaces, should be appropriate for the developmental level of the children. In general, older preschool children and kindergarten children need longer paths.

▲ The dice should involve quantities appropriate for both the length of the path and the developmental levels of the children. Young preschoolers typically use one 1-3 die, while older preschool and kindergarten children may use one to two standard 1-6 dice.

▲ The path should be clear and not confusing.

▲ The game should be attractive and durable.

▲ The movers should correlate with the topic of the game.

▲ Illustrations and print should be neat and relevant to the game.

What pitfalls should teachers avoid?

Path games will be most successful if teachers consider the following:

▲ Spaces should not touch each other. This makes it difficult for children to count as they move.

▲ The movers should not cover more than one space at a time. Otherwise the children will be confused as they attempt to quantify the spaces of the path.

▲ Avoid movers with wheels. Children tend to roll them along the path instead of quantifying one space at a time.

▲ Teachers should measure the area where the game will be used to be certain that the game board will fit.

▲ The decorative detail should not make the board cluttered or confusing.

How should path games be displayed?

A math game table is an ideal place for children to use path games. A "math center" can stimulate children's interest in math games, similar to the way "writing centers" increase their attention to written language.

Children can play short path games on the floor or on a low bench, but long path games are too large to fit easily into the manipulative area. Children become frustrated if others step on game boards or knock over movers. Therefore, a game table is preferable for long path games. Children and parents often use the game table as a transitional activity upon arrival or at departure.

How can teachers use path games as assessment tools?

Path games provide teachers with further opportunities to assess children through observation. Teachers can use the same assessment form for path games that they use to record anecdotal data from math manipulatives and grid games. (See the assessment form examples in chapter 2 and the appendix, section A.) They can use the "comments" section to record additional information such as "re-counts space already occupied."

Path Game
Activities

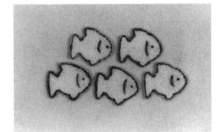

5.1 Doctor Short Path Game

Materials
▲ poster board, 12 by 18 inches
▲ 20 round bandages (⅞ inch) to form two separate paths, each with 10 spaces
▲ illustrations of a doctor's bag at the end points
▲ 2 small wooden or plastic children to use as movers
▲ 1-3 spinner or die

Child's Level
This game is most appropriate for children who can quantify to three and are beginning to use a die or spinner to determine how many spaces to advance along a path. The path is straight and very clear. The spinner may be easier than a die for younger children.

What to Look For
Children may use the spinner and advance an equivalent number of spaces.
Some children will play with the people and hop along the path in a random manner.
Some children may use the spinner but advance without regard to the quantity shown.

Modification
Add bandages to collect at the end of the path.

Helpful Hint

Mount bandage collection pieces on cardboard before laminating.

Questions to Extend Thinking
How do you know how many spaces to move?
If you roll a two, will you reach the doctor bag?
How many more do I have to move before I reach my doctor bag?

Integrated Curriculum Activities
Include doctor books such as *Betsy and the Doctor* by Gunilla Wolde (Random House, 1978), *My Doctor* by Harlow Rockwell (Macmillan, 1973), and *The Lady with the Alligator Purse* by Nadine Westcott (Joy St. Books, 1988) in the reading area.
Create a bandage collection (activity 3.12).
Add the bandage long path game (activity 5.13), if appropriate for your group.
Set up a doctor area in the dramatic-play area.

5.2 Jewel Short Path Game

Materials

- ▲ 2 pieces of poster board, each 6 by 18 inches
- ▲ 18 self-adhesive circles (¾ inch) to form two separate paths, each with 9 spaces
- ▲ crown illustrations at the end points
- ▲ 10 marble chips to use as movers
- ▲ 1-3 die or spinner

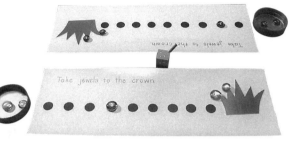

Child's Level

This game is most appropriate for children who can quantify to three and are comfortable advancing along the path according to the amount shown on the die. The additional movers create more complexity for children who are transitioning from short path to long path games.

What to Look For

Children may advance along the path according to the roll of the die.

Some children will repeat the process of advancing marble chips until they cover all five points of the crown.

Some children may place marble chips on the path spaces as they would with a grid.

Modifications

Change to a 1-6 die if a 1-3 die is too easy.

Use different colors of marble chips to encourage comparisons between players.

Questions to Extend Thinking

How many jewels do you want to take to the crown?

How many more jewels will you need to place one on each point of the crown?

Do we both have the same amount of jewels?

Integrated Curriculum Activities

Include the books *King Bidgood's in the Bathtub* by Audrey Wood (Harcourt Brace Jovanovich, 1985) and *Grandma's Jewelry Box* by Linda Milstein (Random House, 1992) in the reading area.

Create a jewel collection (activity 3.11) or a ring collection (activity 3.14).

Include the "Jewels for a Crown" grid game (activity 4.12) in the manipulative area.

Add the castle long path game (activity 5.17), if appropriate for your group.

Helpful Hints

The die shown in the photograph was made from a cube-shaped top.

Use metallic circles to make an interesting path.

The crowns will be attractive if they are made from glittery paper.

5.3 Teddy Bear Short Path Game

Book

This game is designed to coordinate with *A Pocket for Corduroy* by Don Freeman (Viking Press, 1978).

Rubber stamp pictures of Corduroy, copyright Don Freeman for Kidstamps, 1993

Materials

▲ poster board, 12 by 18 inches
▲ 20 paw print stickers to form two separate paths, each with 10 spaces
▲ rubber stamp imprints of Corduroy at the start points
▲ 2 large 2-inch buttons for the end points
▲ a selection of buttons in a small box for children to collect at the end points
▲ 2 small bears, each a different color, to use as movers
▲ 1-3 die or spinner

Child's Level

This game is most appropriate for children who can quantify to three and are beginning to use a die to determine the number of spaces to advance along a path. The collection of buttons creates an additional dimension and provides more opportunities for children to consider other mathematical relationships such as comparing or quantifying their buttons. It also encourages them to play the game many times to get more buttons!

Helpful Hints

Color the Corduroy stamp impressions with markers.

Encourage parents to donate buttons.

What to Look For

Children may advance along the path according to the amount shown on the die.

Some children will play with the buttons and group them by attributes of interest to them.

Some children may place one button on each space of the path as they would with grid games.

Children may return to the start after each game to play again
and collect more buttons.

Some children will count or compare the quantities of buttons
they collect.

Modifications

Change to a 1-6 die if a 1-3 die is too easy.

Eliminate the buttons to make the game less complex.

Kindergarten children may be interested in graphing the buttons
they collect at the end of the game.

Questions to Extend Thinking

How many more spaces do you need to move to reach the buttons?

Do we each have the same amount of buttons? How can we find out?

What do I have to roll to get to the button box?

Integrated Curriculum Activities

Include the books *Corduroy* by Don Freeman (Viking Press, 1968)
and *The Button Box* by Margarette S. Reid (Dutton Children's
Books, 1990) in the reading area.

Create a button collection (activity 3.2).

Include the teddy bear grid game (activity 4.7) in the manipulative
area.

Add the teddy bear long path game (activity 5.14), if appropriate
for your group.

Sew with burlap and large plastic needles.

5.4 Balloon Short Path Game

Materials

- ▲ poster board, 12 by 22 inches
- ▲ 20 balloon stickers to form two separate paths, each with 10 spaces
- ▲ silhouette stickers for the start points
- ▲ party stickers (cake, streamers, hat) for the end points
- ▲ basket of tiny hats to collect at the end points
- ▲ 2 small wooden or plastic people to use as movers
- ▲ 1-3 die or spinner

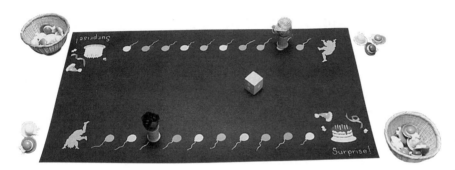

Child's Level

This game is most appropriate for children who can quantify to three and are using a die to determine the number of spaces to advance along a path. The path is short and straight, but the balloon stickers and added illustrations may distract children who are inexperienced.

What to Look For

Children may advance along the path based on the amount shown on the die.

Some children will use the small people to pretend to go to a party and will disregard the die.

Some children will advance to the end of the path and collect hats. Some will repeat the cycle to collect more hats.

Modifications

Change to a 1-6 die if a 1-3 die is too easy.

Eliminate the hat collection to make the game less complex.

Kindergarten children may wish to graph the hats they collect.

Questions to Extend Thinking

Who is closer to the party, you or your friend? How do you know?

How many more spaces do you need to move to reach the party?

If you roll a two, will you reach the party?

Have you each collected the same amount of hats?

Helpful Hint

If there are children in the class who do not celebrate birthdays, make the end point of the game a house instead of a party.

Integrated Curriculum Activities

Include party books such as *Mary Wore Her Red Dress* by Merle
   Peek (Clarion Books, 1985), *Happy Birthday Sam* by Pat
   Hutchins (Viking Penguin, 1981), and *My Presents* by Rod
   Campbell (Macmillan, 1989) in the reading area.

Include the balloon grid game (activity 4.18) in the manipulative
   area.

Add the balloon long path game (activity 5.23), if appropriate for
   your group.

Use balloons for a gross-motor or creative-movement activity.

5.5 Chicken Short Path Game

Predictable Book
This game is designed to coordinate with *Rosie's Walk* by Pat Hutchins (Macmillan, 1986), in which Rosie the hen is chased by a fox on her way to the chicken coop.

Materials
- ▲ poster board, 12 by 18 inches
- ▲ 18 self-adhesive circles (⅜ inch) to form two separate paths, each with 9 spaces
- ▲ rubber stamp imprints of the Fox at the start points
- ▲ chicken coop illustrations at the end points
- ▲ small containers of corn to collect at the end points
- ▲ 2 small hens to use as movers
- ▲ 1-3 corn spinner

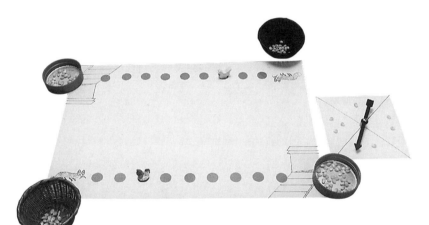

Rubber stamp pictures of the Fox, copyright Pat Hutchins for Kidstamps, 1993

Child's Level
This game is most appropriate for children who can quantify to three and are comfortable advancing along a path according to the amount shown on the spinner. The unique spinner and corn to collect at the end of the path increase the complexity of a short path game as children transition toward long path games.

What to Look For
Children may advance along the path based on the amount shown on the spinner.

Some children will play the game several times to collect corn each time they reach the end of the path.

Some children may use the spinner to collect corn but not to advance along the path.

Some children may advance to the end of the path but not collect the corn.

Some children may count or compare quantities of corn.

Some younger children may use the path spaces like a grid game and simply place a piece of corn on each circle.

Modification

Try using Indian corn (colored) with a corresponding spinner to designate which color of corn to take.

Questions to Extend Thinking

How many pieces of corn can the hen collect?

How many spaces does the hen have to move to get away from the fox?

Is the hen just as close to the chicken coop as the fox? How can you tell?

Integrated Curriculum Activities

Read the big book *Rosie's Walk* (Scholastic, 1987) with the children.

Include *Rosie's Walk* in the reading area.

Include the chicken grid game (activity 4.15) in the manipulative area.

Add the farm long path game (activity 5.15), if appropriate for your group.

Put corn with scoops and clear buckets in the sensory table.

Helpful Hints

The fox may be more attractive if it is colored in.

You can make the corn spinner by dividing a square of poster board into fourths and gluing on the corn. Insert a one-inch paper fastener through the spinner, then through a small bead, and finally through the poster board to mount the spinner. (The bead allows the spinner to rotate above the corn.)

5.6 Letter Short Path Game

Book

This game is designed to coordinate with *A Letter to Amy* by Ezra Jack Keats (Harper Row, 1968), in which a little boy writes a letter to invite a friend to his birthday party. On the way to the mailbox, he drops the letter as the wind blows during a rainstorm.

Materials

- ▲ 2 pieces of poster board, each 6 by 18 inches
- ▲ 20 envelope and letter stickers to form two separate paths, each with 10 spaces
- ▲ silhouette stickers for the start points
- ▲ mailbox illustrations for the end points
- ▲ two wooden or plastic people to use as movers
- ▲ 1-3 die or spinner

Child's Level

This game is most appropriate for children who can quantify to three and are just beginning to play short path games. The path is straight, short, and very clear.

What to Look For

Children may advance along the path according to the roll of the die.

Some children may hop along the path to the mailbox without regard to the amount shown on the die.

Modifications

Add more people movers to encourage children to move along the path several times.

Change to a 1-6 die if a 1-3 die is too easy.

Provide small pieces of paper at the end of the path for children to write letters or their names.

Helpful Hint

Use white correction fluid to create the lightning.

Questions to Extend Thinking

How many more spaces do you have to move to mail your letter?
If I move two more, will I be just as close to the mailbox as you are?
What do you need to roll to reach the mailbox?

Integrated Curriculum Activities

Include the books *The Jolly Postman* by Janet and Allan Ahlberg (Little, Brown, 1986) and *A Letter to Amy* in the reading area.

Share rain and wind songs with the children.

Include the letter grid game (activity 4.10) in the manipulative area.

Add the letter long path game (activity 5.16), if appropriate for your group.

Set up a pulley in the gross-motor area so children can mail letters (activity 7.12).

5.7 Autumn Short Path Game

Materials
- ▲ 2 pieces of poster board, each 6 by 18 inches
- ▲ 20 self-adhesive circles (¾ inch) to form two separate paths, each with 10 spaces
- ▲ 2 squirrel stickers for the end points
- ▲ 2 large acorns, mounted on wooden disks so they will not roll, to use as movers
- ▲ 1-3 die or spinner

Child's Level
This game is most appropriate for children just beginning to play path games using a 1-3 die. The path is straight, short, and clear.

What to Look For
Children may advance along the path according to the roll of the die.
Some children will hop along the path without regard to the die.
Some children may repeat the cycle of advancing along the path to feed the squirrel again and again.

Modifications
Provide more acorns to carry to the squirrel.
Add other types of nuts for variety.

Helpful Hint

Younger children may bring acorns from the nut collection to use with the short path game. Perhaps the two activities can be placed in separate areas of the room.

Questions to Extend Thinking
How do you know how many spaces to move?
If you roll a two, will you reach the squirrel?
How many acorns does your squirrel have?

Integrated Curriculum Activities
Include autumn books such as *Nuts to You!* by Lois Ehlert (Harcourt Brace Jovanovich, 1993) in the reading area.
Create a nut collection (activity 3.15).
Select an autumn long path game (activity 5.12 or 5.18) that is appropriate for your group.
Plan a nut tasting activity.
Take a nature walk.
Plan a nut and leaf collage as an art activity.
Put large nuts, tongs, and buckets in the sensory table.

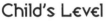5.8 Planting Short Path Game

Predictable Book
This game is designed to coordinate with *The Carrot Seed* by Ruth Krauss (Harper/Festival, 1973) in which a little boy cares for the carrot seed he planted.

Materials
- ▲ 2 pieces of poster board, each 6 by 18 inches
- ▲ 18 self-adhesive circles (¾ inch) to form two separate paths, each with 9 spaces
- ▲ wheelbarrow stickers for the start points
- ▲ carrot illustrations for the end points
- ▲ 2 small watering cans to use as movers
- ▲ 1-3 die or spinner

Child's Level
This game is most appropriate for children just beginning to play path games using a 1-3 die. The path is short, straight, and very clear.

What to Look For
Children may advance along the path according to the roll of the die.
Some children may use the watering cans in a dramatic-play manner to water the plants.
Some children will advance along the path without regard to the amount shown on the die.

Modifications
Use small trowels or people as movers.
Change to a 1-6 die if a 1-3 die is too easy.

Questions to Extend Thinking
How many more do you need to roll to water the plant?
How many times will you water your plant?
If I roll a one, will my watering can be as close to the plant as yours?

Integrated Curriculum Activities
Include other planting books such as *Growing Vegetable Soup* by Lois Ehlert (Harcourt Brace Jovanovich, 1987) in the reading area.
Add the planting long path game (activity 5.19), if appropriate.
Make vegetable soup or carrot raisin salad with the children.
Add watering cans to the sensory table.
Plant seeds, indoors or outdoors.
Set up a flower shop in the dramatic-play area.
Plan a seed collage as an art activity.

Helpful Hints

Look for small erasers in the shape of watering cans. Craft stores may sell miniature watering cans for doll houses.

Use small carrot erasers as collection pieces to extend the game.

5.9 Treasure Chest Short Path Game

Materials
- ▲ poster board, 12 by 18 inches
- ▲ 16 squares (2 inches) with gold stars in the centers to form two separate paths, each with 8 spaces
- ▲ small treasure boxes for the end points
- ▲ 20- to 40-piece collection of junk jewelry to use as movers
- ▲ 1-4 die

Child's Level
This game is most appropriate for children who have had many experiences playing grid and short path games with large quantities of counters. The use of a 1-4 die and 20 to 40 pieces of jewelry add complexity to the game as children transition toward longer path games.

Helpful Hints

Use jewels from the jewel collection in place of junk jewelry.

Look in fabric stores or craft stores for small gold-tone and silver-tone charms to substitute for junk jewelry.

What to Look For
Children may roll the die and advance a piece of jewelry toward or away from the treasure chest.

Some children will count or compare the quantities of jewelry they remove from or put into the chest.

Modification
Reduce the number of pieces of jewelry if the initial amount is too overwhelming.

Questions to Extend Thinking
How can the jewelry be divided so each player starts with the same amount?

How many more silver pieces than gold pieces do you have?

Do you have as many gold pieces as I do?

How many pieces will you have in your chest if you take one out?

Integrated Curriculum Activities

Include the book *Grandma's Jewelry Box* by Linda Milstein (Random House, 1992) in the reading area.

Create a jewel collection (activity 3.11) or a ring collection (activity 3.14).

Add the treasure chest long path game (activity 5.20), if appropriate for your group.

Set up a beach in the dramatic-play area, with sand in a small wading pool and shells hidden in the sand.

5.10 Winter Short Path Game

Materials

- ▲ poster board, 12 by 18 inches
- ▲ 14 snowflake stickers to form two separate paths, each with 7 spaces
- ▲ silhouette stickers for the start points
- ▲ snowmen stickers for the end points
- ▲ small counters (sunglasses, hats, brooms, and carrot erasers) to collect for the snowmen
- ▲ 2 people movers
- ▲ 1-3 die or spinner

Child's Level

This game is most appropriate for children who have played numerous short path collection games. The path is shorter than most because the child must repeat the cycle from start to finish several times in order to collect all the snowman components.

What to Look For

Children may advance along the path according to the roll of the die.

Some children will advance along the path several times to collect items for the snowman.

Some children will move along the path randomly without regard to the amount on the die.

Modification

Change to a 1-6 die if a 1-3 die is too easy.

Helpful Hint

Use dark poster board for the game boards. It highlights the snowflake stickers.

Questions to Extend Thinking

How many times will you need to go from start to finish to collect all the pieces for your snowman?

How many more spaces do you have to move until you can collect the hat?

Which item should you collect first? Second?

Integrated Curriculum Activities

Include winter books such as *The Snowy Day* by Ezra Jack Keats (Viking Press, 1962), *The Mitten* adapted by Jan Brett (G. P. Putnam's Sons, 1989), and *The Jacket I Wear in the Snow* by Shirley Neitzel (Greenwillow, 1989) in the reading area.

Share winter songs and poems with the children.

Create a snowflake collection (activity 3.16).

Include the snowman grid game (activity 4.8) or a snowflake grid game (activity 4.11 or 4.16) in the manipulative area.

Add the winter long path game (activity 5.21), if appropriate for your group.

Spray-paint snow with colored water.

Add winter word cards to the writing area.

Put a snowflake rubber stamp in the art area.

5.11 Apple Short Path Game

Materials

▲ 2 pieces of poster board, 6 by 22 inches
▲ 20 apple stickers to form two separate paths, each with 10 spaces
▲ basket stickers for the end points
▲ 2 apples to use as movers
▲ 1-3 die or spinner

Child's Level

This game is most appropriate for children just beginning to play short path games. The game can also be used by more advanced players when several apple movers are available for each player.

What to Look For

Children may advance along the path according to the roll of the die.

Some children will repeat the cycle with additional apples when available.

Some children may hop along the apple path from start to finish without regard to the die.

Some children may count or compare the quantities of apples taken to the basket.

Younger children may place apples in one-to-one correspondence on the path spaces as they would with a grid.

Modifications

Provide more apple movers to encourage children to continue playing the game.

Use different colors of apple movers for variety.

Change to a 1-6 die if a 1-3 die is too easy.

Helpful Hint

Look for red and yellow apples on garlands in craft stores or paint wooden apples two different colors.

Questions to Extend Thinking

How many more spaces will you need to move to reach the basket?
If you roll a one, will you reach the basket?
How many more apples will you take to the basket?
Do we each have the same amount of apples in our baskets?

Integrated Curriculum Activities

Include the book *Apples and Pumpkins* by Anne Rockwell
(Macmillan, 1989) in the reading area.

Share apple songs and poems with the children.

Add the apple long path game (activity 5.22), if appropriate for
your group.

Cook applesauce with the children.

Take a field trip to pick apples.

Wash apples in the sensory table or in tubs.

Sort real apples by size, type, and color.

Taste apples and graph the results (activity 6.5).

5.12 Autumn Continuous Path Collection Game

Materials
▲ poster board, 15 by 15 inches
▲ 24 self-adhesive circles (¾ inch) to form a continuous path
▲ 5 basket stickers for collection spaces
▲ basket of 25 to 50 acorns for collection pieces
▲ 2 small squirrel movers, each a different color
▲ 1-6 die

Child's Level
This game is most appropriate for children who can quantify to six and have had experiences with short path games and larger quantities of counters.

What to Look For
Children may move along the path according to the roll of the die and collect an acorn when the squirrel lands on a basket sticker.

Some children may play with the acorns.

Some children will count or sort the acorns.

Some children will hop the squirrels around the path without regard to the die.

Some children may place one acorn on each circle or place several acorns on each basket.

Modifications
Use two dice for children who are ready for addition.
Provide other types of nuts or seed pods for variety.
Kindergarten children may want to graph how many of each type they collect.

Helpful Hint

Use a glue gun to secure loose acorn caps to the nuts.

Questions to Extend Thinking
What should happen when a squirrel lands on a basket?
How many more spaces do you need to move to reach a basket?
What happens if both squirrels land on the same space?

Integrated Curriculum Activities

Include autumn books such as *Nuts to You!* by Lois Ehlert
 (Harcourt Brace Jovanovich, 1993) in the reading area.

Create a nut collection (activity 3.15).

Select another autumn path game (activities 5.7 or 5.18) that is
 appropriate for your group.

Plan a nut tasting activity.

Take a nature walk.

Put large nuts, tongs, and buckets in the sensory table.

5.13 Bandage Long Path Game

Materials

▲ poster board, 22 by 22 inches
▲ 25 paper squares (2 inches), each with a ¾-inch self-adhesive circle in the center
▲ silhouette stickers for the start of the path
▲ assorted bandages for the end of the path
▲ small wooden or plastic people to use as movers
▲ 1-6 die

Child's Level

This game is most appropriate for children who can quantify to six and are beginning to use long path games. The small number of spaces, clear path, and absence of traps or bonus spaces make this one of the easier long path games.

What to Look For

Children may advance along the path according to the roll of the die.
Some children may hop along the path to the bandages at the end without regard to the die.
Inexperienced children may roll the die, move more spaces than indicated, and quickly advance to the end.

Modifications

Provide an assortment of bandages to collect at the end.
Use a second die for children who are ready for addition.

Questions to Extend Thinking

How many more will you need to move to catch up to your friend?
How many do you need to roll to reach the bandages?

Helpful Hint

Mount bandages to collect at the end of the game on cardboard before laminating.

Integrated Curriculum Activities

Include doctor books such as *Lotta's Bike* by Astrid Lindgren (R & S Books, 1989), *Betsy and the Doctor* by Gunilla Wolde (Random House, 1978), and *My Doctor* by Harlow Rockwell (Macmillan, 1973) in the reading area.

Create a bandage collection (activity 3.12).

Include the doctor short path game (activity 5.1) for children not yet ready for long path games.

Set up a doctor's office in the dramatic-play area.

5.14 Teddy Bear Long Path Game

Book

This game is designed to coordinate with *A Pocket for Corduroy* by Don Freeman (Viking Press, 1978), in which a small bear is lost in the laundromat as he searches for a pocket.

Materials

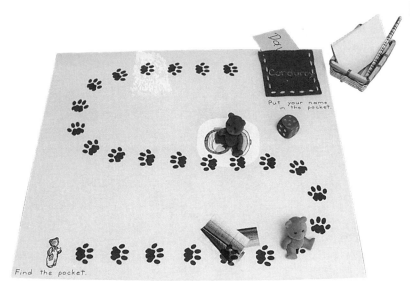

Rubber stamp pictures of Corduroy, copyright Don Freeman for Kidstamps, 1993

- ▲ poster board, 22 by 22 inches
- ▲ 25 bear paw stickers to form the path
- ▲ rubber stamp imprint of Corduroy for the start of the path
- ▲ illustrations of towels, a clothes dryer, and soap flakes for possible trap/bonus spaces
- ▲ a felt pocket as the finish space
- ▲ 2 or more small figures of bears, each a different color, to use as movers
- ▲ slips of paper for children to write their names on and insert into the pocket at the end of the game
- ▲ 1-6 die

Child's Level

This game is most appropriate for children who have had experience playing short path games and perhaps some long path games such as the bandage path game (activity 5.13). Children may perceive the illustrations as traps or bonus spaces.

What to Look For

Children may use the die to determine how many spaces to advance.

Some children may retell the story as they advance the bear movers in a random way.

Some children will generate guidelines for the paw prints that cross the illustrations of the towels, clothes dryer, and soap flakes.

Modification

Use two dice for children who are ready for addition.

Questions to Extend Thinking

How many more spaces do you need to move to reach the soap flakes?

What happens if you land on the paw print at the clothes dryer?

What do you need to roll to get past the towels?

If you roll a three, will you reach the pocket?

Integrated Curriculum Activities

Include the books *A Pocket for Corduroy* and *Corduroy* by Don Freeman (Viking Press, 1968) and *The Button Box* by Margarette S. Reid (Dutton's Children's Books, 1990) in the reading area.

Create a clothespin collection (activity 3.6).

Include the teddy bear short path game (activity 5.3) for children not yet ready for long path games.

Create a class graph—Do your clothes have pockets or not?

Helpful Hints

Use pictures from advertisements or wallpaper books for the towels.

Use catalog pictures for the clothes dryer.

Use white correction fluid to make the soap flakes.

The stamp impression is attractive when colored with markers.

Be sure the bear paw stickers cross over the illustrations if you want the children to view them as traps or bonus spaces.

5.15 Farm Long Path Game

Predictable Book
This game is designed to coordinate with *Rosie's Walk* by Pat Hutchins (Macmillan, 1986), in which Rosie the hen is chased by the Fox on her way to the chicken coop.

Materials
- ▲ poster board, 22 by 22 inches
- ▲ 36 self-adhesive circles (¾ inch) to form the path
- ▲ rubber stamp imprints of Rosie and the Fox at the start points
- ▲ bee stickers
- ▲ illustrations of a chicken coop, a pond, and a haystack
- ▲ basket of corn to collect each time around the path
- ▲ a small hen and a small fox, or two small hens, to use as movers
- ▲ 1 or 2 standard 1-6 dice, or a corn spinner

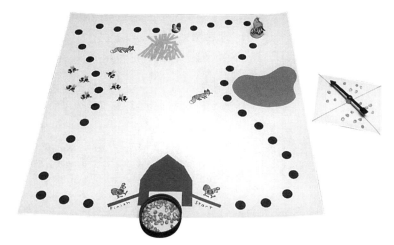

Child's Level
This game is most appropriate for children who can quantify to at least six and are ready for a longer, more complex path with pieces to collect at the end. Children who are ready for addition can use two dice.

Rubber stamp pictures of Rosie and the Fox, copyright Pat Hutchins for Kidstamps, 1993

What to Look For
Children may use the spinner or dice to determine how many spaces to move along the path.

Some children may move the fox and hen along the path and retell the story.

Some children will generate rules related to the illustrations based on the story line.

Some children will ignore the illustrations next to the path and will not include them in the rules for play.

Some children will collect corn at the end of each round and count or compare the amount they each have.

Modification

Provide a third die for children who are ready for more challenging addition.

Questions to Extend Thinking

How many spaces do you have to move to get away from the Fox?
How will you decide how many pieces of corn to collect at the end?
How many more spaces do you have to move until you get away from the bees?

Integrated Curriculum Activities

Read the big book *Rosie's Walk* (Scholastic, 1987) with the children.
Add the chicken grid game (activity 4.15) to the manipulative area.
Include the chicken short path game (activity 5.5) for children not yet ready for long path games.
Put corn with scoops and clear buckets in the sensory table.
Make prints with corn cobs and paint.
Add farm animals to the block area.

Helpful Hints

The illustrations of Rosie and the Fox are most attractive when colored with markers.

Use construction paper or magazine illustrations to represent the pond, haystack, and chicken coop.

You can make the corn spinner by dividing a square of poster board into fourths and gluing on the corn. Insert a one-inch paper fastener through the spinner, then through a small bead, and finally through the poster board to mount the spinner. (The bead allows the spinner to rotate above the corn.)

5.16 Letter Long Path Game

Book

This game is designed to coordinate with *A Letter to Amy* by Ezra Jack Keats (Harper Row, 1968), in which a little boy writes a letter to invite a friend to his birthday party. On the way to the mailbox, he drops the letter as the wind blows during a rainstorm.

Materials

- ▲ poster board, 22 by 22 inches
- ▲ 40 self-adhesive circles (¾ inch) to form the path
- ▲ 3 envelope stickers for traps ("oops!" spaces)
- ▲ illustrations of a mailbox, lightning, and raindrops
- ▲ an assortment of party stickers (hats, streamers, birthday cake) for the end of the game
- ▲ small plastic or wooden people to use as movers
- ▲ 2 standard 1-6 dice

Child's Level

This game is most appropriate for children who have had many experiences playing long path games. The path is more challenging than in some of the other games due to the added illustrations and the more obvious trap spaces. The use of a standard pair of dice is appropriate for children who are ready to add two dice.

What to Look For

Children may roll one die and advance along the path according to the amount shown.

Children may roll two dice and add them together by counting all the dots before moving along the path.

Some children will ignore the "oops!" trap spaces on the path.

Some children will generate rules for the "oops!" spaces and the mailbox space.

Modification
Put a miniature mailbox on the mailbox illustration and add slips of paper so children can write messages and mail them as they walk by the mailbox.

Questions to Extend Thinking
What should you do when you land on the "oops!" spaces?

How many more spaces do you have to move before you can reach the mailbox?

How many will you need to roll to get past the next "oops!" space?

What happens when you land on the mailbox?

Integrated Curriculum Activities
Include the books *The Jolly Postman* by Janet and Allan Ahlberg (Little, Brown, 1986) and *A Letter to Amy* in the reading area.

Share rain and wind songs with the children.

Add the letter grid game (activity 4.10) to the manipulative area.

Include the letter short path game (activity 5.6) for children not yet ready for long path games.

Set up a pulley in the gross-motor area so children can mail letters (activity 7.12).

Helpful Hints

Use white correction fluid to create the lightning.

Use a magazine photograph for the mailbox or take a photograph of a local mailbox to decorate the board.

5.17 Castle Long Path Game

Predictable Book

This game is designed to coordinate with *King Bidgood's in the Bathtub* by Audrey Wood (Harcourt Brace Jovanovich, 1985), in which the Page tries to get the King out of the tub, where he stays all day.

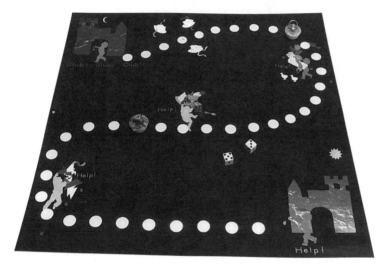

Materials

- ▲ poster board, 22 by 22 inches
- ▲ 39 self-adhesive circles (¾ inch) to form the path
- ▲ 5 silhouette stickers to represent the Page along the path
- ▲ illustrations of a castle for the start and the finish
- ▲ 2 rubber sink stoppers, each a different color, to use as movers (idea by Susan Thorpe)
- ▲ 2 standard 1-6 dice

Child's Level

This game is most appropriate for children who have had experiences with long path games and are ready for intriguing trap or bonus spaces that are more obscure than those in activities 5.16 or 5.23. The addition of a second die allows children to add the dice together when they are ready.

Helpful Hint

Use permanent markers to color the stoppers so players can distinguish their own movers.

What to Look For

Children may roll one or two dice to determine how far to advance along the path.
Some children will generate rules for the Page trap/bonus spaces.
Some children will ignore the Page spaces.
Some children will add two dice together by counting all the dots.

Modification

Add collection pieces, such as small fruits and vegetables or rubber worms, at the Page trap/bonus spaces.

Questions to Extend Thinking

What should happen when a player stops at the Page?

How many more do you need to move to catch up to your friend?

What do you need to roll to avoid the Page?

Do you have to roll the exact number of spaces to reach the end?

How many more spaces do you have to move before you reach the Page again?

Integrated Curriculum Activities

Include the books *Grandma's Jewelry Box* by Linda Milstein (Random House, 1992) and *King Bidgood's in the Bathtub* in the reading area.

Create a jewel collection (activity 3.11) or a ring collection (activity 3.14).

Add the "Jewels for a Crown" grid game (activity 4.12) to the manipulative area.

Include the jewel short path game (activity 5.2) for children not yet ready for long path games.

Plan a glitter or sequin collage as an art activity.

Build a bathtub with large blocks in the dramatic-play area.

5.18 Autumn Long Path Game

Materials

- ▲ poster board, 22 by 22 inches
- ▲ 42 self-adhesive stickers (¾ inch) to form the path
- ▲ illustrations of acorns for collection spaces
- ▲ oak tree sticker for the end of the game
- ▲ squirrel sticker to begin the game
- ▲ 2 small squirrels, each a different color, to use as movers
- ▲ 2 standard 1-6 dice
- ▲ a basket of acorns to collect at the end of the game or when a player lands on an acorn space

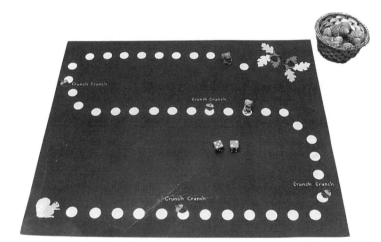

Child's Level

This game is most appropriate for children who are ready for a longer path and are secure using one or two standard dice. They may begin adding combinations of dots on the dice.

What to Look For

Children may roll one or two dice to determine how far to move along the path.

Some children will hop the squirrels randomly along the path.

Some children will add two dice together by counting all the dots.

Some children may ignore the acorn collection spaces on the path.

Some children will generate rules for what happens when players land on the acorn spaces.

Some children will collect acorns at the end of the game.

Some children will count or compare quantities of acorns collected.

Helpful Hint

Use stickers for the acorns if you have trouble drawing them.

Modifications

Provide additional types of nuts for variety.
Kindergarten children may wish to graph the nuts they collect.

Questions to Extend Thinking

If you want to miss the acorn space, what will you have to roll?
How do you decide how many acorns to collect at the end?
How many do you need to roll to catch the other squirrel?

Integrated Curriculum Activities

Include autumn books such as *Nuts to You!* by Lois Ehlert
   (Harcourt Brace Jovanovich, 1993) in the reading area.

Create a nut collection (activity 3.15).

Select another autumn path game (activities 5.7 or 5.12) that is
   appropriate for your group.

Plan a nut tasting activity.

Take a nature walk.

Plan a nut and leaf collage as an art activity.

Put large nuts, tongs, and buckets in the sensory table.

5.19 Planting Long Path Game

Predictable Book
This game is designed to coordinate with *The Carrot Seed* by Ruth Krauss (Harper/Festival, 1973) in which a little boy cares for the carrot seed he planted.

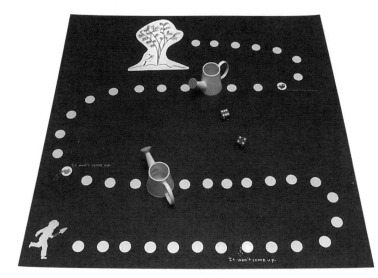

Materials
- poster board, 22 by 22 inches
- 44 self-adhesive circles (¾ inch) to form the path
- a silhouette sticker for the start of the game
- illustration of a plant for the end of the game
- illustrations of watering cans for trap/bonus spaces
- 2 small watering cans, each a different color, to use as movers
- 2 standard 1-6 dice

Child's Level
This game is most appropriate for children who are comfortable using a longer path and generating rules for trap/bonus spaces. The addition of a second die allows children to add the dice together when they are ready.

What to Look For
Children may roll one or two dice to determine how far to move along the path.
Some children will disregard the quantities on the dice and move randomly along the path.
Some children will add two dice together by counting all the dots.
Some children will ignore the trap/bonus spaces.
Some children will generate positive or negative rules for the trap/bonus spaces.

Helpful Hint

A silver paint marker can be used to draw the watering cans on the trap/bonus spaces.

Modifications

Provide a third die for children who are ready for more challenging addition.

Small carrot erasers can be added to collect at the end of the game. Children can quantify them and compare the results.

Questions to Extend Thinking

How many spaces will you need to move to water the first carrot?

Can you reach the next watering space in only one roll of the dice?

If you roll a double, will you reach the next bonus space?

What happens when you land on a watering can?

Integrated Curriculum Activities

Include the books *Growing Vegetable Soup* by Lois Ehlert (Harcourt Brace Jovanovich, 1987) and *The Carrot Seed* in the reading area.

Create a grid with watering cans (activity 4.19).

Include the planting short path game (activity 5.8) for children not yet ready for long path games.

Make vegetable soup or carrot raisin salad with the children.

Add watering cans to the sensory table.

Plant seeds, indoors or outdoors.

Set up a flower shop in the dramatic-play area.

Plan a seed collage as an art activity.

5.20 Treasure Chest Long Path Game

Materials
▲ poster board, 22 by 22 inches
▲ 50 star stickers to form the path
▲ illustration of a castle for the end of the game
▲ small wooden or plastic people to use as movers
▲ treasure box and junk jewelry or jewels to collect
▲ 2 standard 1-6 dice

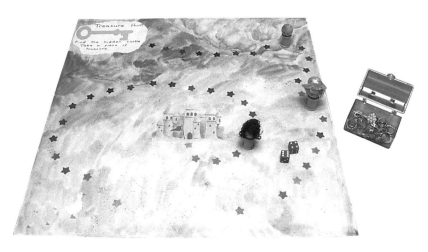

Child's Level
This game is most appropriate for children who are very comfortable playing path games of 40 to 50 spaces. The path is slightly camouflaged since the game is a treasure hunt. The large numbers of collection pieces and the pair of dice add complexity as well.

What to Look For
Children may roll one or two dice to determine how far to advance along the path.

Some children will take a jewel each time they reach the treasure chest at the end of the path.

Some children may advance to the treasure chest and then reverse direction to return to the start.

Some children will add the dice by counting all the dots.

Some children will count and compare quantities of treasure.

Modification
Reduce the number of jewelry pieces to collect if the original amount is too overwhelming.

Questions to Extend Thinking
How do you know how many pieces of jewelry to collect at the end?
How many more spaces will you need to move to get to the treasure?
If you skip the gold stars, how far will you advance on this turn?

Helpful Hint

Be sure to establish a ground rule as to when the jewelry should be returned, whether at the end of the game or the end of the day. If the jewelry is to be returned at the end of each day, children will search for all the pieces. This is also a math activity!

Integrated Curriculum Activities

Include the book *Tough Boris* by Mem Fox (Harcourt Brace, 1994) in the reading area.

Create a jewel collection (activity 3.11) or a ring collection (activity 3.14).

Include the treasure chest short path game (activity 5.9) for children not yet ready for long path games.

Set up a beach in the dramatic-play area, with sand in a small wading pool and shells hidden in the sand.

Plan a glitter or sequin collage as an art activity.

Sew large beads or spangles on burlap.

5.21 Winter Long Path Game

Materials
▲ poster board, 22 by 22 inches
▲ 49 self-adhesive circles (¾ inch) to form the path
▲ construction paper and stickers (carrot, scarf, hat, and coal) for the bonus spaces
▲ snowman sticker at the end of the game
▲ 2 small felt boards, 6 by 8 inches
▲ felt pieces (2 each of a snowman, hat, carrot, and scarf; multiple pieces of coal)
▲ small wooden or plastic people to use as movers
▲ 2 standard 1-6 dice

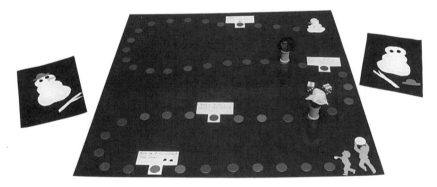

Child's Level
This game is most appropriate for children who have played complex path games and enjoy trap/bonus spaces. The bonus spaces require some knowledge of addition combinations. Older preschool and kindergarten children find this game challenging.

Helpful Hints

Be prepared for younger children to ignore the path game and simply play with the felt board pieces for an extended period. After that, a well-timed question may draw their attention to the game.

Children who cannot yet read will remember the bonus directions because they are so unique.

What to Look For
Children may roll one or two dice to determine how far to move along the path.

Some children will advance along the path but ignore the bonus space directions, for example, "roll an 8 to collect the scarf."

Some children will advance along the path with the intent of landing on the bonus spaces. They may change direction just to return to a bonus space they missed, or they may choose not to move until they finally roll the number they need to land on a bonus space.

Some children will add two dice together by counting all the dots.

Some children will ignore the dice and play with the flannelboard pieces.

Modifications

Due to the complexity of this game, no modifications are recommended. Give ample time for children to explore possibilities.

Questions to Extend Thinking

What do you need to roll to reach the first bonus space?
How many ways can you roll a twelve to collect the hat?
What happens if you advance past the bonus space without stopping?
How do you get your carrot if you miss the carrot space?

Integrated Curriculum Activities

Include winter books such as *The Snowy Day* by Ezra Jack Keats (Viking Press, 1962), *The Mitten* adapted by Jan Brett (G. P. Putnam's Sons, 1989), and *The Jacket I Wear in the Snow* by Shirley Neitzel (Greenwillow, 1989) in the reading area.
Share winter songs and poems with the children.
Create a snowflake collection (activity 3.16).
Include the snowman grid game (activity 4.8) or a snowflake grid game (activity 4.11 or 4.16) in the manipulative area.
Include the winter short path game (activity 5.10) for children not yet ready for long path games.
Estimate how many snowmen are in a clear plastic jar.

5.22 Apple Long Path Game

Materials
- ▲ poster board, 22 by 22 inches
- ▲ 43 paper squares (1½ inch) to form the path
- ▲ 8 apple stickers with holes or bites out of them for the trap/bonus spaces
- ▲ index cards, with quantities of dots from 1 to 10, to draw after each move to determine how many marble chips to take
- ▲ 50 or more red marble chips in a small basket to collect at the end of the path
- ▲ small wooden or plastic people to use as movers
- ▲ 2 standard 1-6 dice

Child's Level
This game is most appropriate for kindergarten children who have had many experiences with long path games and with quantifying large amounts of objects. The path is long and there are many trap/bonus spaces with directions. The two dice encourage addition.

What to Look For
Children may roll one or two dice to determine how far to advance along the path.

Children may draw a card to determine how many marble chips to take.

Some children will advance along the path and collect one marble chip each time they land on a bonus space.

Some children will generate rules for traps and bonus spaces before the game is played.

Modification
Use colored index cards with directions such as "collect 24 apples," which children can draw at the beginning of the game.

Questions to Extend Thinking

What should happen when a player lands on a trap or bonus space?

How many do you need to roll to miss the trap?

How many more chips do you need to collect to have the amount on your card?

Integrated Curriculum Activities

Include the book *Apples and Pumpkins* by Anne Rockwell (Macmillan, 1989) in the reading area.

Share apple songs and poems with the children.

Include the apple short path game (activity 5.11) for children not yet ready for long path games.

Cook applesauce with the children.

Take a field trip to pick apples.

Wash apples in the sensory table or in tubs.

Sort real apples by size, type, and color.

Taste apples and graph the results (activity 6.5).

Helpful Hints

If children do not think about the traps and bonus spaces, try asking questions such as—

Should we take chips or put chips back when we land on an apple with a hole in it?

Should something different happen when we land on an apple with a bite out of it?

If this type of game follows many experiences with the other games described in this chapter, children will have an understanding of traps and bonus spaces.

5.23 Balloon Long Path Game

Materials
- ▲ poster board, 22 by 22 inches
- ▲ 27 paper squares (2 inches), each with a balloon sticker, with some balloons cut apart and "Pop!" written on the square
- ▲ silhouette stickers for the start
- ▲ party hat, streamer, and birthday cake stickers for the finish
- ▲ small wooden or plastic people to use as movers
- ▲ 1-6 die

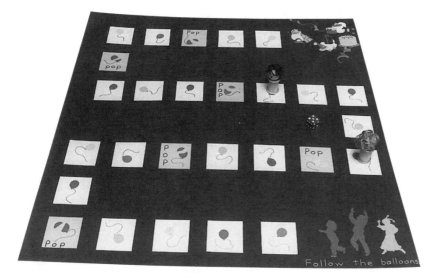

Child's Level
This game is most appropriate for children who can quantify to six and have had some experience playing long path games without definite traps. The popped balloons may encourage children to consider generating some "rules" for play.

Helpful Hint
Metallic paint markers work well for lettering and drawing strings on the balloons.

What to Look For
Children may use the die to determine how many spaces to advance. Some children may move from start to finish in a random manner. Some children may ignore the popped balloons. Some children will determine rules for the popped balloons.

Modification
Use a second die for children who are ready for addition.

Questions to Extend Thinking

How many more do you need to move to catch up to your friend?

What will you need to roll to get past the popped balloon?

What do you think should happen if a player lands on a popped balloon?

Integrated Curriculum Activities

Include party books such as *Mary Wore Her Red Dress* by Merle Peek (Clarion Books, 1985), *Happy Birthday Sam* by Pat Hutchins (Viking Penguin, 1981), and *My Presents* by Rod Campbell (Macmillan, 1989) in the reading area.

Add the balloon grid game (activity 4.18) to the manipulative area.

Include the balloon short path game (activity 5.4) for children not yet ready for long path games.

Use balloons for a gross-motor or creative-movement activity.

Interactions with Path Games

ANECDOTE 1

Edward (age 4½) played a teddy bear long path game (activity 5.14) with his teacher. He used one 1-6 die. Each time Edward rolled the die, he counted the number of dots and then counted the same number of spaces along the path. The exception was six. Each time Edward rolled a six, he correctly counted six dots but moved only five spaces. The teacher thought she could help by calling attention to this. She said, "I heard you count to six on the die, but you counted only five spaces when you moved your teddy bear." After hearing this comment, Edward began fixing the die so that he never got higher than three. The teacher realized that her subtle correction caused him to regress in the level of difficulty he was willing to encounter.

ANECDOTE 2

Laura (age 4½) played a long path game using two standard 1-6 dice. The teacher noticed that Laura added the two dice together by counting all the dots; however, she did not count all the dots on one die before continuing on to the second die. Instead, Laura counted some of the dots on the first die, then the dots on the second die, and then moved back to the first die again. When it was her turn, the teacher modeled counting all the dots on the first die, then on the second die. Laura continued to quantify in her own manner.

The teacher conjectured that Laura did not view the dice as separate sets that she was combining. The teacher gave Laura two very different-appearing dice to see if this would cause Laura to view the dice as separate sets. The next time they played, the teacher used one regular die and one large blue die. Laura now added the dice together by counting all the dots on the first die before continuing on to the second die. After two weeks of using the unusual die in combination with the standard die, the teacher returned to using two standard dice. The teacher noted that Laura now counted all the dots on the first die before adding on the dots from the second die, even with identical dice. The teacher speculated that using the two different-appearing dice had helped Laura construct the concept of the dice being separate sets that she added together to get the total.

ANECDOTE 3

Beth and Andre (both 4½ years old) played a farm long path game (activity 5.15) together. They used two standard 1-6 dice. When Andre took his turn, he counted the number of dots on the first die and moved that number of spaces before counting the number on the second die and moving that amount. Beth, on the other hand, counted the dots on both dice together and then moved the total number of spaces required. Beth said to Andre, "You don't have to count the dice like that. You can just count them all together." Andre did not reply and continued quantifying the dice separately. Two weeks later the teacher noted that Andre had begun to add two dice together by counting all the dots before moving on the path.

CHAPTER 6

Graphing

- ▲ Which month has the most class birthdays?

- ▲ Which animal was the most popular on the zoo trip?

- ▲ Are there more children in our class who have had chicken pox or more who have not had it?

These questions interest young children. The questions inspire them to think deeply about important mathematical concepts. Whole-math teachers use real class situations such as these to stimulate mathematical reasoning. The use of class bar graphs to record the necessary data to answer such questions has emerged as a regular component of our math curriculum with older preschool and kindergarten children.

Teachers' Questions

What are class graphs?

Class graphs are bar graphs carefully designed to help children record class voting responses. Constance Kamii in *Number in Preschool and Kindergarten* (NAEYC, 1982; p.50) suggests voting as useful in promoting children's autonomy and in encouraging them to compare quantities. We have found that recording their votes on a bar graph helps children visualize the quantities involved and facilitates making comparisons. The graph preserves the votes so that children can continue to count, compare, and discuss the results long after the initial voting has concluded. Having the opportunity to continue thinking about a mathematical problem aids in the construction of mathematical concepts.

Teachers must remember that graphing is a step removed from comparing two sets of objects. The children's selections are transformed into paper symbols, which are then sorted into groups. Graphing is difficult; many preschool and even more kindergarten children, however, do construct concepts of graphic representation. Teachers should expect wide variations in children's processing skills with graphs.

Why is it important to include graphs in the math curriculum?

Class graphs provide yet another opportunity for children to create and compare sets. Since children are excited to see the results of their voting, they often think about more difficult math problems than they typically would. For example, they may begin to construct subtraction concepts as they try to decide how many more votes their column needs to catch another column.

What makes a good graph?

A good graph clearly displays information that is of high interest to the class. Older preschool and kindergarten children become increasingly aware that their peers may have views that differ from their own. They become interested in class voting to see what everyone thinks about a popular topic. A good graph arises out of the children's natural desire to share information with their peers, quantify the results, and compare the outcomes. Graphs can be especially motivating to cognitively advanced children since they provoke a high level of thinking.

What is wrong with commercial graphs?

Commercial graphs appear in many kindergarten workbooks. They are usually of no interest whatsoever to the children! Who really cares how many red fish and how many blue fish are on the work sheet? On the other hand, visualizing how many children have brought back field trip permission slips and how many have not (activity 6.9) could be really important!

What mathematical concepts emerge as children use class graphs?

Graphs can facilitate the construction of classification skills, one-to-one correspondence, quantification, set comparisons, addition, and subtraction.

Each child's choice is transferred onto the graph into the appropriate column. Children eagerly watch the placement of each vote. They see that all the children who make the same choice are grouped together. Thus, graphing strongly reinforces ideas of classification. Children also note that there is one bar on the graph for each child's vote. This reinforces concepts of one-to-one correspondence.

Children are eager to quantify as the graphs emerge. They want to know how many votes their column has. They look to see which column has the most. They chuckle about rows that have few or no votes, and they become excited if one column begins catching up with another.

Children tackle difficult concepts of addition and subtraction on graphs because they are eager to know the answers. If two columns are tied, it becomes important to speculate about how the addition of the votes of two absent children could affect the outcome. If a column is catching up to their column, they will wrestle with subtraction strategies to find out how many they are ahead by. Comparing the final tallies is also of interest as children eagerly relate to their parents or friends how many more votes one group has than another. It is amazing how long children will persist with difficult problems when the results really matter to them.

What are some criteria to consider when making graphs?

▲ *Always graph from bottom to top.* Children are accustomed to making height comparisons of familiar things such as block towers, people, buildings, or animals. Many children become confused if the graph starts at the top and goes down since the rows all appear to be the same height.

▲ *Use clear pictures and/or words at the bottom of each column to indicate which votes will go in each row.*

▲ *Children are more interested in graphs if they can remember how each person voted.* Print the children's names on slips of paper to go onto the graph or let the children write their own names in their own ways.

▲ *Be sure the tags are carefully aligned.* Otherwise, a column with fewer votes may look taller than a column with more votes. The graph can be gridded to make vote placement easier. Children can write directly onto laminated graphs.

▲ *Allow enough space in each column to record all of the possible votes.* Sometimes a large number of children select the same item!

▲ *Select a topic that is truly interesting to the children.* Otherwise, they will not be motivated to think about the math. Graphs that correlate with a class unit are often effective.

▲ *Graphs for younger preschool children should be very personal,* for example, boy or girl, hair color, or eye color. Choosing a favorite character from a book or remembering a favorite animal from a field trip is too abstract for many younger children.

What are some pitfalls to avoid?

▲ *Do not put contact paper over permanent marker.* It makes the marker "bleed." Use a watercolor marker under contact paper. Either type of marker can be used with lamination.

▲ *When voting, avoid asking the entire group for a show of hands.* Young children tend to vote for every choice. For example, if the teacher asks how many like chocolate ice cream the best (activity 6.2), all the children are likely to raise their hands. If she then asks how many like strawberry the best, many children may again raise their hands. Instead, ask the children individually which one they vote for.

▲ *Be aware of the hidden ramifications of the topic you select.* For example, having children vote on what they ate for Thanksgiving stigmatizes children who do not celebrate Thanksgiving for cultural or socioeconomic reasons. A vacation graph may embarrass children who do not take vacations. Similarly, a pet graph may sadden children who don't have a pet, or it may anger their parents.

▲ *Avoid racial stereotyping.* For example, a teachers' activity book on Native Americans suggests having children vote on whether they would rather herd sheep, make jewelry, or weave rugs if they were a Navajo. This suggests to children that these are the only things Navajos do!

▲ In late preschool and kindergarten "winning," or voting in the column that ends up with the most votes, often dominates the voting. This may actually discourage autonomy. When this happens, the teacher can quietly approach the children one-by-one prior to group time and record their choices. The responses can then be graphed during group time.

What is the teacher's role?

The teacher is a facilitator and mediator. He can direct children to focus on particular math concepts through his questions. Some suggestions for questions to stimulate thinking appear below. Also, check the activity pages for specific questions related to each graph.

▲ Which one has the most votes so far?

▲ Which one has the fewest?

▲ What would happen if this row got one more vote? Two more?

▲ How many more votes does this row have than this one?

Children may disagree on their assessment of the results of the graph. The teacher can encourage children to continue thinking by remaining neutral. Rather than saying that one answer is right and another wrong, she can ask other children for their opinions and ask children to justify their responses.

Sometimes peer pressure becomes intense. The teacher can reassure children that there is no winner. The teacher may also decide to vote herself so that she can model voting for a column that does not have the most votes. Appropriate comments to de-emphasize winning include:

▲ Different people like different things.

▲ It's okay to make a different choice from your friend.

▲ This one has the most votes, but I like this one the best.

▲ The one I voted for has fewer votes than the one Jayhawk chose.

How can teachers assess children's math skills through their use of graphs?

Teachers should not expect preschool and kindergarten children to be able to graph independently. Rather, they can observe children as they discuss the graphs and record what information the children deduce from the graph. For example, can they tell which column has the most votes, which has the fewest, or if two columns are the same? Some children can figure out how many more votes a particular column would need in order to equal another.

Leave the graphs up for several days. Children like to think about these questions over time and discuss them. They also like to point out the results to visitors or family members.

Why are so many group graphs used instead of individual graphs?

Group graphs enable children to work collaboratively. Children have an opportunity to learn from each other. As children make errors, other children may disagree or challenge them. Being questioned by another child may create disequilibrium, that is, cause a child to question previously held beliefs. This often leads to a change in thinking. Repeated experiences with group graphs provide a foundation for later experiences with individual graphs.

Are individual graphs ever used?

Individual graphs are used with kindergarten children who have had numerous experiences with group graphs. (See activity 6.10 and anecdote 3 for an example of an individual-graph activity.)

Graphing
Activities

6.1 Hair Color Graph

Description

This graph reinforces identity issues. Each child decides which column is closest to his or her hair color.

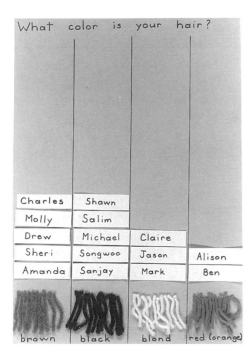

Materials

- ▲ poster board or paper, 12 by 18 inches or a size large enough to accommodate all of the children's decisions, laminated or covered with clear contact paper
- ▲ 2-inch pieces of yarn, in colors that represent the children's hair color (black, brown, red, yellow), to identify each column of the graph
- ▲ a name tag for each child
- ▲ tape to attach name tags to the chart

Child's Level

This is a good beginning graph for young preschoolers because it is so concrete. They can readily observe each other's hair color. Older preschoolers and kindergartners also enjoy graphing hair color.

What to Look For

Children may count to quantify how many people have each color of hair.

Children may compare column heights to determine whether there are more, fewer, or the same number of name tags for each hair color.

A few children may subtract to determine how many more name tags one column has than another.

Young preschool children may focus only on their own names.

Helpful Hint

On this graph children have to approximate since most hair colors will not exactly match the samples. This challenges the rigid thinking of the preoperational child.

Questions to Extend Thinking

Which color is your hair most like?

Does anyone's hair match exactly?

What will happen when Marla comes back? (This question is asked because two columns are tied.)

Integrated Curriculum Activities

Include the book *Straight Hair, Curly Hair* by Augusta R. Goldin (Crowell, 1966) in the reading area.

Set up a beauty parlor in the dramatic-play area.

6.2 Favorite Ice Cream Graph

Description
Each child chooses one favorite ice cream flavor, and the selections are then graphed. Instead of bars, this graph uses circles so that the columns look like giant ice cream cones.

Materials

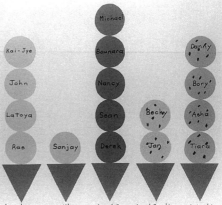

strawberry   vanilla   chocolate   chocolate chip   mint chip

▲ poster board or paper, 18 by 16 inches or a size large enough to accommodate all of the children's decisions, laminated or covered with clear contact paper
▲ brown construction paper cut into cone shapes to form the base of each column
▲ name tags made from construction paper circles in colors to represent the ice cream flavors
▲ tape to attach name tags to the chart

Child's Level
Both preschool and kindergarten children like talking about ice cream. For younger preschoolers, this activity should follow an ice cream tasting experience to make it more concrete.

What to Look For
Children may count to quantify how many votes each flavor of ice cream received.
Children may compare column heights to determine whether there are more, fewer, or the same number of votes for each flavor.
A few children may subtract to determine how many more votes one column has than another.
Children may vote for the flavor that seems to be "winning."

Questions to Extend Thinking
What is the most popular flavor?
Which flavor has the fewest votes?
How many more votes does chocolate have than strawberry?
Are there any flavors that have the same number of votes?

Integrated Curriculum Activities
Read the poem "Bleezer's Ice Cream," from *The New Kid on the Block* by Jack Prelutsky (Greenwillow Books, 1984) to the children.
Make ice cream with the children.
Put ice cream flavor word cards in the writing center.
Add ice cream cone blank books to the writing center.
Set up an ice cream shop in the dramatic-play area.

Helpful Hints

The day before you plan to graph, ask the children individually to pick a favorite flavor. Then you will know which flavors to include on the graph.

If your class is selecting a flavor prior to making ice cream, be sure it is clear that everyone gets to eat the ice cream, even if their flavor is not selected.

6.3 Shoe Fastener Graph

Description
Children always seem to be interested in their shoes. For this graph they are asked how their shoes fasten. This graph was used in connection with a shoe unit built around *I Went Walking* by Sue Williams (Harcourt Brace Jovanovich, 1989).

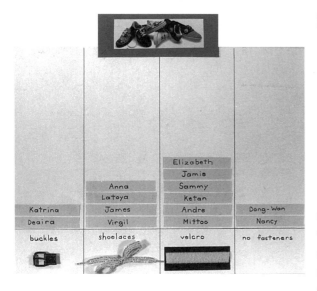

Materials
▲ poster board or paper, 22 by 16 inches or a size large enough to accommodate all of the children's decisions, laminated or covered with clear contact paper
▲ a small buckle, a shoelace bow, and a piece of Velcro, to identify each column
▲ a name tag for each child
▲ tape to attach name tags to the chart

Child's Level
This is a good beginning graph for preschoolers who are very interested in their own shoes. Kindergartners also like this graph and enjoy changing the results each day to correspond to their shoes.

What to Look For
Children may count to quantify how many people have each type of shoe fastener.

Children may compare column heights to determine whether there are more, fewer, or the same number of name tags for each type of shoe fastener.

A few children may subtract to determine how many more name tags one column has than another.

Some children may incorrectly record their type of shoe fastener in order to be in the same column as a friend.

Questions to Extend Thinking
What is the most common type of shoe fastener in our class?
How many people have shoelaces?
How many more people have laces than have buckles?

Helpful Hint

Laminate the chart first and then attach the shoe fasteners.

Integrated Curriculum Activities

Include the books *New Blue Shoes* by Eve Rice (Macmillan, 1975), *Shoes* by Elizabeth Winthrop (Harper & Row, 1986), and *I Went Walking* in the reading area.

Create a shoe collection (activity 3.3).

Try shoe printing using small key chain shoes or novelty shoes.

Make footprints by painting the children's feet and allowing them to walk along a strip of paper.

Set up a shoe store in the dramatic-play area.

6.4 Author Unit Graph

Description

This graph is a concluding activity for a Pat Hutchins author unit, which includes *The Doorbell Rang* (Greenwillow Books, 1986), *Titch* (Macmillan, 1971), *Changes Changes* (Macmillan, 1986), *Rosie's Walk* (Macmillan, 1986), *Good-Night Owl* (Macmillan, 1972), and *The Wind Blew* (Macmillan, 1974). The children know all the books well and vote for their favorite one.

Materials

▲ poster board or paper, 18 by 12 inches or a size large enough to accommodate all of the children's decisions, laminated or covered with clear contact paper
▲ teacher-made illustrations to represent each book
▲ a name tag for each child
▲ tape to attach name tags to the chart

The Doorbell Rang	Titch	Changes Changes	Rosie's Walk	Good-Night Owl	The Wind Blew
	Jared		Nancy		Dale
	Tiara	Andy	Drew	Jason	Shiraz
Asha	Claire	Mikey	Mikey	Sangwoon	Elizabeth

Child's Level

This topic is more abstract than topics such as hair color or shoes. Therefore, this graph is more appropriate for older preschool and kindergarten children and should follow experiences with more concrete graphs.

Helpful Hint

It is easier for children to add or subtract when comparing adjacent rows. Take this into consideration when formulating questions to stimulate problem solving.

What to Look For

Children may count to quantify how many votes each book received.

Children may compare column heights to determine whether there are more, fewer, or the same number of votes for each book.

A few children may subtract to determine how many more votes one column has than another.

Children may vote for the book that seems to be "winning."

Questions to Extend Thinking

Did any of the books receive the same number of votes?

What will happen if Karen votes for *Good-Night Owl* when she comes back?

How many more votes does *Titch* have than *The Doorbell Rang?*

How many more votes does *Titch* have than *Changes Changes?*

Integrated Curriculum Activities

Include books by Pat Hutchins in the reading area.

Read big book versions of *Rosie's Walk* (Scholastic, 1987), *The Wind Blew* (Scholastic, 1974), and *The Doorbell Rang* (Scholastic, 1988) to the children, but not all on the same day.

Include chicken path games (activities 5.5 and 5.15) in the manipulative area, if appropriate for your group.

Put character word cards from the books in the writing center.

6.5 Apple Tasting Graph

Description
Children taste three types of apples, Granny Smith, Red Delicious, and Golden Delicious, and select their favorite. The results are recorded on a graph.

Rayshawn	Leslie	
	Daniel	
	Bruce	
Ben	Kelley	Lakesha
Celia	Lilly	Vince
Abbey	Ping	Shandra
Zach	Christopher	James
Red Delicious	Golden Delicious	Granny Smith

Materials
- ▲ red, yellow, and green strips of paper mounted on poster board, 12 by 18 inches, to form columns for the apple choices
- ▲ an apple-shaped cutout mounted at the bottom of each column
- ▲ a name tag for each child
- ▲ tape to attach name tags to the chart

Child's Level
Older preschool and kindergarten children are intrigued with taste differences and are excited about this graph. Young children, on the other hand, seem to have difficulty selecting a favorite apple and thus are less interested in this graph.

What to Look For
Children may want to vote for more than one apple.

Children may count to quantify how many votes each type of apple received.

Children may compare column heights to determine whether there are more, fewer, or the same number of votes for each apple.

A few children may subtract to determine how many more votes one column has than another.

Questions to Extend Thinking
Which is the most popular kind of apple?

How many votes does Golden Delicious have?

Do more people like Granny Smith or Red Delicious?

What would happen if one more person voted for Red Delicious? Two more?

Helpful Hint

During apple tasting, many children like to have a scarf tied over their eyes so that they can't see what they're tasting. However, children should *never* be blindfolded against their will.

Integrated Curriculum Activities

Include the book *Apples and Pumpkins* by Anne Rockwell
(Scholastic, 1989) in the reading area.

Add apple path games (activities 5.11 and 5.22) to the manipulative area, if appropriate for your group.

Set up a farmers' market in the dramatic-play area.

Cook applesauce or make fruit salad with the children.

Sing apple songs and read apple poems.

Take a field trip to pick apples.

Wash apples in the sensory table or tubs.

Sort a collection of apples by size, type, and color.

6.6 Pumpkin Growing Prediction Chart

Description

This chart is used prior to a field trip to a pumpkin farm. It encourages children to follow the scientific procedure of forming a hypothesis, collecting data, and checking their hypothesis. Children predict whether pumpkins grow on a tree (like an apple), on a bush (like berries), under the ground (like carrots), or on a vine (like grapes). On the field trip, the children check their hypotheses.

How do you think pumpkins grow?

Sarah			
Steven		Patty	
Chad		Ronnie	
Mark	Robin	Jimmy	
Amanda	Ruby	Trey	Audrey
Jeff	Eric	Barb	Peter
on a Tree	on a bush	under ground	on a vine

Materials

▲ poster board or paper, 12 by 18 inches or a size large enough to accommodate all of the children's decisions, laminated or covered with clear contact paper
▲ illustrations of pumpkins growing on a tree, a bush, under the ground, and on a vine at the bottom of the columns
▲ a name tag for each child
▲ tape to attach name tags to the chart

Child's Level

This graph is most appropriate for older preschool and kindergarten children since it involves prediction and more abstract subject matter.

What to Look For

Most city children do not know where pumpkins grow and therefore have to guess.
Children may want to change their predictions after the field trip.

Helpful Hint

Be sure to look at the graph again after the field trip. Emphasize that scientists also make guesses (hypotheses) to help direct their observations. Scientists also often make wrong guesses!

Questions to Extend Thinking

How many children predict that pumpkins grow on trees? (Repeat for the other columns.)
Which column has the most votes?
Which column has the fewest?
How will we find out how pumpkins grow?

Integrated Curriculum Activities

Include the book *Pumpkin Pumpkin* by Jean Titherington (Greenwillow Books, 1986) in the reading area.

Make pumpkin bread or roast pumpkin seeds with the children.

Plan a seed collage for the art area.

Allow children to guess the number of vertical grooves on a pumpkin (idea by Nora Cordrey).

6.7 Chicken Pox Graph

Description
Chicken pox becomes an important topic of discussion during late winter and early spring as children begin to contract it. On this graph, children can compare how many of them have or have not had the chicken pox. The graph can be used in conjunction with the book *Betsy and the Chicken Pox* by Gunilla Wolde (Random House, 1976).

Have you had the chicken pox?

	MAS
	kaβ-JYe
	LELa
	mmm
	MoMoKo
M	NIKK)
DORIT	Eric
AACHEL	Dwir
EMILY	mmm
ADDISON	YUJEY
Yes	No

Materials
▲ poster board or paper, 12 by 18 inches or a size large enough to accommodate all of the children's decisions, laminated or covered with clear contact paper
▲ drawings of a child with and without chicken pox at the bottom of the columns
▲ a permanent marker for children to write their names on the graph

Child's Level
This graph is appropriate for older preschool and kindergarten children who notice when their peers get the chicken pox. Young children don't necessarily know what chicken pox is.

What to Look For
Children may count to quantify how many have had chicken pox and how many have not.
Children may compare column heights to determine whether more people have or have not had chicken pox.
Some children may subtract to determine how many more name tags one column has than another.

Helpful Hint

Send notes home ahead of time so that parents can confirm whether or not their child has had the chicken pox.

Questions to Extend Thinking
Have more children in our class had the chicken pox or not had the chicken pox?
How many children have had the chicken pox?
How many children have not had the chicken pox?
How many more children have not had the chicken pox than have had the chicken pox?

Integrated Curriculum Activities

Include the books *When Daddy Had the Chicken Pox* by Harriet
   Ziefert (Harper Collins, 1991) and *Betsy and the Chicken Pox* in
   the reading area.
Create a bandage collection (activity 3.12).
Select a doctor path game (activity 5.1 or 5.13) that is appropriate
   for your group.
Set up a doctor area in the dramatic-play area.
Plan face painting activities with washable watercolor crayons.

6.8 Favorite Character Graph

Description
Children vote for their favorite main character, the Page or the King, from *King Bidgood's in the Bathtub* by Audrey Wood (Harcourt Brace Jovanovich, 1985).

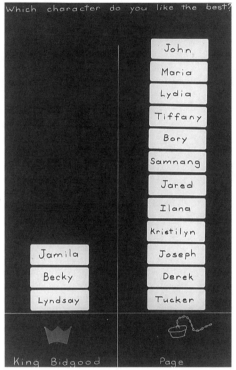

Materials
▲ poster board or paper, 12 by 18 inches or a size large enough to accommodate all of the children's decisions, laminated or covered with clear contact paper
▲ illustration of a sink stopper and a crown to represent each character
▲ a name tag for each child
▲ tape to attach name tags to the chart

Child's Level
This graph is suitable for older preschool and kindergarten children who have had many graphing experiences and enjoy discussing their choices. Character selection is too abstract for most young preschoolers.

What to Look For
Children may count to quantify how many votes each character received.

Children may compare column heights to determine whether the Page or the King has more votes.

A few children may subtract to determine how many more votes one character has than another.

Children often vote for the character that seems to be "winning."

Helpful Hint

In the photo, the Page has so many more votes than the King that there may be too large a difference for the children to handle a subtraction question.

Questions to Extend Thinking
Who has more votes, King Bidgood or the Page?
How many votes did King Bidgood get?
How many votes did the Page get?
Maria, what did you like about the King?
Samnang, what did you like about the Page?

Integrated Curriculum Activities

Include *King Bidgood's in the Bathtub* and other books by Audrey Wood, such as *The Napping House* (Harcourt Brace Jovanovich, 1984) and *Quick as a Cricket* (Child's Play, 1982), in the reading area.

Put rubber bait worms and fish nets in the water table.

Create a jewel collection (activity 3.11).

Select path games based on the King Bidgood theme (activities 5.2 and 5.17), if appropriate for your group.

6.9 Recording Permission Slips

Description
This graph has a practical purpose. It records data on who has or has not returned field trip permission slips. The mathematical thinking changes as more slips are brought in.

```
 Zoo   Permission    Slips

 Shiraz
 Andy
 Mikey
 Elizabeth
 Drew              Sangwoon
 Claire            Dale
 Molly             Jason
 Nancy             Asha
 Tiara             Jared
 Thisara           Daniel

 Yes               Not Yet
```

Materials
▲ poster board or paper, 12 by 18 inches or a size large enough to accommodate all of the children's decisions, laminated or covered with clear contact paper
▲ a sample permission slip to mark one column
▲ a name tag for each child
▲ tape to attach name tags to the chart

Child's Level
Field trips are a part of many early childhood programs, and collecting permission slips is a significant part of the process. Therefore, both preschool and kindergarten children are interested in this graph.

What to Look For
Children may count to quantify how many people have turned in their permission slips and how many have not.

Children may compare column heights to determine whether more people have or have not turned in their permission slips.

Some children may want to record daily changes in the graph.

Questions to Extend Thinking
How many permission slips have been brought back?
How many people have not yet returned their permission slips?
How many permission slips will we have when everyone brings one back?

Integrated Curriculum Activity
Allow children to take attendance by hanging name tags on an attendance chart.

Helpful Hint

This graph could be recreated on a magnetic bulletin board and used for many field trips.

6.10 Individual Graph

Description
Each interested child receives a bag with various kinds of crackers or pretzels. The children use graph paper to record their quantities of food in their own way.

Materials
- ▲ individual bag of food for each child with:
  2 to 5 goldfish crackers
  2 to 5 teddy bear crackers
  2 to 5 small pretzels
- ▲ 1-inch graph paper with illustrations of the food at the bottom of each column

Child's Level
This graph is most appropriate for kindergartners who have had many experiences with group graphs.

What to Look For
See anecdote 3 at the end of this chapter for examples of individual graphs.

Questions to Extend Thinking
How can you represent this food on your paper so we can remember what was in the bag?
Which food do you have the most of?
How can I tell from your graph how much of each food you have?

Integrated Curriculum Activities
Add the "Salty Pretzel" Book (activity 2.25) to the reading area.
Set up a grocery store in the dramatic-play area.
Allow children to vote for their favorite food item (goldfish crackers, teddy bear crackers, or pretzels) on a group graph.
Make soft pretzels with the children.

Helpful Hint

Quantities larger than 5 per food type might be too difficult for young children to deal with when graphing.

Many children will need to align the actual food on the graph paper. Be careful to allow children to graph in their own way. Telling them a "right way," that is, your way, teaches them a trick but does not help them construct math knowledge.

Interactions with Graphs

ANECDOTE 1

A preschool class had spent the morning tasting three types of apples: red, yellow, and green. At group time the teacher discussed which of the three kinds of apples each child had liked the best. As the apple conversation was nearing a close, the teacher asked if there was a way to find out which apple was the most popular.

Alice soon came up with a suggestion. She said, "Get red, yellow, and green paper. Put all the people that liked red apples on the red paper, all the people that liked yellow apples on the yellow paper, and all the people that liked green apples on the green paper. Then we can tell." The teacher altered her plan for the rest of group time so that the class could immediately follow Alice's suggestion and graph the apples.

Alice had obviously constructed the mathematical concept of the use of a graph. She selected graphing as a way to compare the apple-tasting results. This is how the apple graph described in activity 6.5 originated.

ANECDOTE 2

A class of mostly four-year-olds voted for their favorite farm animals after a field trip. Five people voted for the horse, four for the sheep, three for the cow, two for the pig, one for the chicken, and no one for the goose. The teacher recorded each child's vote on a bar graph. When he asked which animal had received the most votes, many children said "the horse." When the teacher asked which had received the fewest votes, several children said "the chicken." No one suggested the goose.

Preschool children have difficulty considering sets of zero when they make comparisons. The response of this class was typical.

ANECDOTE 3

During a summer pre-kindergarten class, the children were each given a bag containing goldfish crackers, vanilla teddy bear crackers, and chocolate teddy bear crackers. There were one to five crackers of each type in each child's bag. The children were encouraged to represent what was in their bag on the graph paper so that everyone could remember what each child had had even after all the crackers had been eaten. However, they were not told how to make the graph.

The examples show different ways that children represented the food on their graphs. All six children had constructed mathematical concepts that enabled them to symbolically represent the crackers. However, many different levels of knowledge are evident.

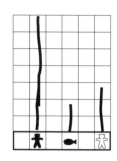

▲ Philip lined up his crackers in the appropriate columns. He put one cracker in each box in consecutive order from bottom to top. Philip then drew a vertical line through the boxes to show how high each row was. He drew his lines correctly through the columns containing two or three crackers, but he made a long line to the top of the page for the column containing five bears.

Children can often handle new concepts when using small quantities but not larger ones. Thus, Philip could graph quantities of two and three, but not five.

▲ Kenan colored in blocks to correspond to the number of each type of cracker in his bag. He used the same color of marker as the color of cracker; he did not, however, line up the blocks in columns.

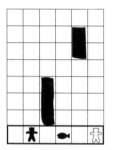

Kenan has constructed the concepts of one-to-one correspondence and classification when graphing. He does not yet understand the idea of grouping data in columns for comparison.

▲ Douglas lined up his crackers, one per box, in the appropriate columns. He put hash marks at the top of each column to indicate how many had been in each row.

Douglas understands the idea of grouping his data in columns, but he does not yet realize that the number of boxes used in each column also quantifies his data. He therefore supplies hash marks to record the amounts of each type of cracker.

▲ Anthony correctly graphed his crackers in appropriate columns. Rather than just coloring in a corresponding number of boxes, **he drew a picture** of the type of cracker he wanted represented in each box.

Although Anthony has correctly graphed his data, he may not yet realize that just coloring in the boxes in the appropriate column is enough information to tell another person which kind of cracker is meant. He therefore feels the need to actually draw each cracker represented.

▲ Heidi also correctly graphed her crackers, but like Anthony she drew a picture of each type of cracker rather than just coloring in the boxes. She also wrote the appropriate numeral at the top of each column to indicate the quantity.

▲ Ping graphed her crackers by coloring in the appropriate number of boxes in each column. She used only one color of marker for the graph. While coloring in her boxes, Ping verbalized that she did not need to change the color of marker to tell how many she had of each type of cracker. She could tell that by looking at the columns. Ping was the only child in the class who realized this.

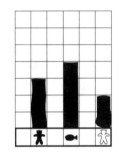

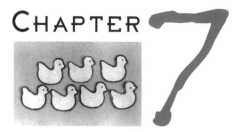

Math And Gross-Motor Play

▲ I knocked down three pins the first time and two pins the second time. That's 1, 2, 3, 4, 5 altogether.

▲ Let's count to three and then we all jump off together!

▲ My note says send two teddy bears and three kitty cats across the pulley.

Children incorporate math as a regular part of their normal gross-motor play. They count as they jump rope or toss and catch a ball. They attempt to keep track of how many baskets they make. They try to throw all of their beanbags into a can. Teachers can capitalize on the math possibilities inherent in gross-motor play and create even more opportunities for children to compare sets, quantify, add, and subtract.

Teachers' Questions

Why should teachers combine math with gross-motor play?

Gross-motor play provides new and additional opportunities for children to think about mathematical relationships.

Scorekeeping is an aspect of many gross-motor games that is not commonly a part of classroom games. It affords children the opportunity to quantify their points, add scores together, and compare their totals with others. Scorekeeping motivates children to stretch their mathematical reasoning.

Counting is a natural outgrowth of gross-motor play. Children love to count as they move their bodies. Thus, the large-motor room or outside play areas may afford teachers the best opportunities to reinforce or extend stable-order counting. Counting as they move their bodies may give children a more concrete sense of one-to-one correspondence.

How can teachers incorporate math into gross-motor play?

Teachers can start by extending and modifying existing games and equipment. Teachers can listen for counting songs or chants that their students use and introduce new ones. They can design gross-motor path games that are similar to the classroom versions. Teachers can also plan target games that incorporate scorekeeping by combining existing equipment with teacher-made or donated items. They can infuse standard pieces of equipment, such as a pulley frame, with math-rich potential. All of these ideas are explored in the activity section of this chapter.

What makes a good gross-motor game?

The best gross-motor games combine physical knowledge with opportunities for quantification.

Physical knowledge is constructed when the child performs some action on an object and observes the outcome. For example, if a child tries to roll a sphere and a cube down a ramp, she quickly observes that the sphere rolls and the cube does not. This is physical knowledge. In physical-knowledge games the child has to adjust her aim, speed, or force to obtain the desired result.

Quantification becomes part of a gross-motor game when children keep score. Children may also roll a die in order to decide how many times to perform a trick, and this too involves quantification.

Gross-motor games should be attractive and durable. Both will encourage continued use.

What is the easiest way to introduce math into gross-motor play?

Look for appropriate opportunities to introduce counting and add a giant die to the environment. Children may want to count jumps on the trampoline, swings while hanging upside down, hops on one foot, or how many times they leap up and ring a bell. They may decide to count to a certain number before they jump off a climber or fall onto a mat. These are all excellent occasions for the teacher to reinforce or extend stable-order counting.

Just adding a giant die to the gross-motor environment attracts children's attention. They can invent numerous games that combine the use of the giant die with actions that involve quantification and creation of sets. For example, if a child rolls a three and hops three times, he has first quantified the dots on the die and then created a set (his hops).

Where can teachers get giant dice?

Teachers can make giant dice by gluing felt circles onto large foam cubes from craft or fabric stores. Inflatable dice or large fuzzy dice can sometimes be purchased in party stores. Look in automotive departments for the dashboard size.

How do children keep score?

Some children keep score mentally, while others like to notate their score. Many children use some sort of mark to indicate each point. Vertical or horizontal hash marks and circles are common. Some children use numerals. Some children like to use an abacus to keep score. Each child can use one row of beads to tally her score. Children can also use teacher-made score sheets as shown in some of the activities.

What is the teacher's role?

The teacher sets up the environment to maximize mathematical possibilities. Some of the equipment is organized to encourage games and quantification. The teacher observes the children's interactions and asks leading questions. She looks for opportunities to inject math into the regular play and facilitates discussion about mathematical issues such as scorekeeping.

How can teachers assess children's math levels through gross-motor games?

Teachers can add children's score sheets to their portfolio assessment files. They can keep anecdotal notes on how each child uses the materials or they can record the results on the same type of forms used for manipulatives. (See the sample assessment forms in chapter 2 and the appendix.)

Gross-Motor Math Activities

7.1 Copy Cat Number Song

Directions

This song can be sung as a planned group-time activity or spontaneously while children are playing. The children can take turns devising tricks for everyone to copy, such as hopping, turning around, or clapping. At the end of each verse, the children count as they perform the tricks.

Materials

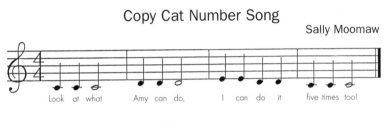

Copy Cat Number Song

Sally Moomaw

Look at what   Amy can do,   I can do it   five times too!

©1993, Sally Moomaw

Child's Level

This game is appropriate for both preschool and kindergarten children. Young children will naturally select easier tricks and smaller quantities. The teacher can also vary the difficulty by suggesting higher quantities.

What to Look For

Children often count in one-to-one correspondence as they perform the tricks.

Some children may not initially know stable-order counting.

Helpful Hint

You can vary the level of the counting depending on the level of the individual child you are playing with or the class as a whole. Thus, if a child already has stable-order counting to three, you might choose to go to five in the song.

Modification

Reduce the number of repetitions, if five are too many.

Questions to Extend Thinking

How many times should we do Nancy's trick?
Can we do one more each time?
How many will we do this time?

Integrated Curriculum Activity

Sing other movement and counting songs (for example, activity 7.2) with the children.

7.2 Ball Counting Song

Directions
The teacher can sing this song as she throws and catches a large ball with a child. At the end of the song, they count the number of catches before the ball is dropped.

Materials
▲ a large ball

Child's Level
This activity is appropriate for older preschool and kindergarten children. Young preschoolers may not yet be able to throw and catch the ball well enough to combine it with counting.

Ball Counting Song

Sally Moomaw

I throw the ball, You throw the ball, How ma-ny times be— fore it falls?

X   X   X
1   2   3 . . .

©1993, Sally Moomaw

What to Look For
Children often count in one-to-one correspondence as they toss and catch the ball.

Some children will keep track of the highest number of catches achieved.

Some children will not be able to count while concentrating on throwing and catching.

Some children will want to count for others as they watch them toss and catch the ball.

Modification
Change the words of the song from "throw" to "bounce" for variety. This also changes the gross-motor skill involved.

Questions to Extend Thinking
How many times do you think we will catch the ball this time?
What is our highest score so far?
How many more catches did we make this time than last time?

Integrated Curriculum Activity
Sing other movement and counting songs (for example, activity 7.1) with the children.

Helpful Hint

This is an excellent, natural opportunity to model stable-order counting.

7.3 People Mover Path Game

Description

Carpet squares are laid out on the floor to form a straight path leading to easel paper, which is taped to the wall. The children are the game movers. They take turns rolling a giant die and hopping along the path. When they reach the end, they can write their names in their own way on the easel paper.

Materials

▲ 10 to 20 carpet squares
▲ giant die
▲ easel paper and pencil or marker

Child's Level

This activity is most appropriate for preschool and kindergarten children who are also playing short path board games in the classroom (see chapter 5).

What to Look For

Children may roll the die and attempt to hop the same number of spaces as dots on the die.

Some children will ignore the die and just hop along the mats.

When playing table-sized path games, many children re-count the square their mover already occupies each time they take a new turn. They often do not make this error when they themselves are the movers.

Helpful Hint

The teacher may need to help retrieve the die. Otherwise, the children will have to leave their spaces on the path to get the die, and they may forget where their spots were.

Modifications

Use 10 carpet squares if 20 are too many.

Reduce the number of dots on the giant die to three if six are too many.

Questions to Extend Thinking

How does Kaitlin know how many to hop?

If Jamie rolls a three, will he pass Kaitlin?

What does Derek have to roll in order to land on Karl's space?

How many does Pam need to reach the end?

Integrated Curriculum Activity

Include short path games in the classroom (see chapter 5).

7.4 Forward And Back

Description
This game is analogous to the classroom short path game. Carpet squares are arranged to form three straight paths of ten mats each leading to a finish line. One child can hop along each path, so one to three children can play at a time. The children take turns drawing from a jumbo deck of cards that tell the children how many spaces to hop forward or backward.

Materials
▲ 30 carpet squares
▲ taped finish line
▲ forward and back jumbo cards, made from 8½ by 11-inch white construction paper, each with 1 to 4 circle stickers and the words "go forward" or "go backward."

Child's Level
This game is most appropriate for older preschool and kindergarten children since it involves more complex directions. Younger children will simplify it to meet their own developmental needs.

What to Look For
Children may follow the directions on the cards and attempt to move a corresponding number of spaces forward or backward along the path.
Some children will disregard the cards and hop along the path in one-to-one correspondence.

Modification
Reduce the number of dots on the cards if four are too many.

Questions to Extend Thinking
How many more do you need to reach the finish line?
If you draw a "go back 1," will you still be ahead of Linda?

Integrated Curriculum Activity
Include short path games in the classroom (see chapter 5).

Helpful Hint

Encourage the children to leave the mats in their prescribed paths at first. Later, when the children are accustomed to gross-motor path games, you may want to suggest that the children use the mats to create their own path games.

7.5 Bear Hunt Game

Description
This game correlates with the traditional "Going on a Bear Hunt" finger play. Giant paw prints are taped to the floor to form a path. The children roll a giant die and hop along the path toward the bear's cave (a box).

Materials
▲ giant paw prints cut out of brown paper, with black construction-paper pads glued on
▲ large wooden or cardboard box
▲ giant die

Child's Level
This game is most appropriate for older preschool and kindergarten children who are playing long path board games in the classroom (see chapter 5). Younger children, however, are excited about the paw prints and may quantify using the die but move randomly along the path as they do in path games.

What to Look For
Children may roll the die and attempt to move the same number of spaces along the path.

Some children will disregard the die and hop along the path in one-to-one correspondence.

Some children may want to hide in the cave and pretend to be the bear. Be prepared for excitement!

Helpful Hint

We tried coloring in the pads on the bear paw prints with a marker, but it is much faster to cut them out of construction paper and glue them on.

Modification
Keep the path simple at first. After the children become familiar with the game, you can increase the difficulty of the path and recreate the story by having it cross a river, go over a bridge, and so on.

Questions to Extend Thinking
If Lela rolls a two, will she have to pass Marisela?
What would Audrey have to roll to be on the same space as Lela?
How many more do you need to reach the cave?

Integrated Curriculum Activities

Include the books *We're Going on a Bear Hunt* by Michael Rosen
(Margaret K. McElderry Books, 1989) and *Blueberries for Sal* by
Robert McCloskey (Viking Press, 1948) in the reading area.

Create the interactive chart for "10 in the Bed" (activity 2.15).

Add teddy bear path games (activities 5.3 and 5.14) to the
manipulative area.

Allow children to dramatize the book *We're Going on a Bear Hunt*
with hand movements.

7.6 Ramp Bowling

Description

This game combines the physical-knowledge properties of a ramp, targeting, and scorekeeping. Create a ramp by using standard gross-motor equipment such as a wide balance beam or plank and a triangular frame, or use a wide wooden board and a hollow block. Allow the children to arrange the bottles at the bottom of the ramp and attempt to knock them down by rolling the ball down the ramp. Have paper and pencil available in case the children want to notate their scores.

Materials

▲ 3 to 10 one-liter plastic bottles
▲ 4-foot wooden board
▲ triangular frame or hollow wooden block
▲ medium-size plastic ball
▲ paper and pencil for scorekeeping

Child's Level

This self-leveling game is appropriate for all ages. Young children may just roll the ball down the ramp, but they are creating important physical-knowledge relationships. Older preschool and kindergarten children are more interested in quantification and scorekeeping.

What to Look For

Children will experiment with where to place the bottles in order to successfully knock them down.

Children will construct relationships between the placement of the bottles and the direction they must aim the ball.

Some children will want to quantify how many bottles they knock down each time. They may use the paper to keep score.

Some children will want to continue playing until they knock down all the bottles.

Helpful Hints

Expect the children to initially be very intrigued with the physical-knowledge aspects of the game.

Scorekeeping may come later.

Modification

Use fewer bottles for younger children.

Questions to Extend Thinking

How many bottles are left?

Is there another way to place the bottles so that more fall down?

I wonder why the ball never hits the bottles on the side.

Integrated Curriculum Activities

Include a table-sized bowling game in the classroom.

Put ramps in the science area with a variety of objects to roll down them.

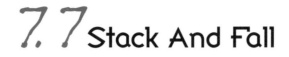

7.7 Stack And Fall

Description
Children stack salt boxes any way they choose and then attempt to knock them down with beanbags. The game encourages quantification (how many boxes fall down), subtraction (how many are left), and the construction of physical knowledge as children explore the stacking properties of the salt boxes and the best strategies for knocking them down.

Materials
▲ 10 empty salt boxes
▲ 3 beanbags
▲ magnetic board with a choice of magnetic discs or numerals for scorekeeping

Child's Level
This self-leveling activity is appropriate for all ages. Young children are usually interested in stacking and knocking down the salt boxes, an important physical-knowledge activity. Older preschool and kindergarten children are more interested in quantification and scorekeeping.

What to Look For
Children will explore a variety of stacking possibilities and observe the results.
Some children will quantify how many they knocked down and how many are left.
Some children will count how many beanbags it takes to knock down all the salt boxes.
Some children will use the magnetic discs or numerals to keep score.

Helpful Hints

Refrain from telling the children how to keep score. If you supply both magnetic discs and numerals, they can select a method appropriate to their level of thinking.

Oatmeal boxes can also be used for this activity.

Modification
For older children, use different-colored boxes and let the children decide how many points each color is worth.

Questions to Extend Thinking
How many boxes fell down?
If you knock one more down, will there be any left?
Is there a way to show how many fell down?

Integrated Curriculum Activity
Use the movement recording *Bean Bag Activities* by Georgiana Liccione Stewart (Kimbo Educational, 1977) with the children.

7.8 Straw-Blowing Cotton Swabs

Description
This game was created after the class had seen a Native American blow dart demonstration. Children aim their straw blowers at a target mounted on the wall and attempt to hit it with cotton swabs. The target helps circumvent potential management problems and encourages scorekeeping.

Materials
- ▲ enough straws for each interested child
- ▲ cotton swabs with one end cut off
- ▲ large, circular target made of three colors of paper or felt
- ▲ paper and pencil

Child's Level
This game is most appropriate for older preschool and kindergarten children. Younger children often have difficulty blowing out through the straw.

What to Look For
Children will explore the physical-knowledge possibilities of directed air.
Some children may decide how many points each circle in the target is worth.
Some children will count one point for each swab that hits the target.
Some children will use the paper to keep a running tally of all their scores.

Modifications
For older children, make a target with more than three concentric circles.
Let older children make their own targets.

Questions to Extend Thinking
How many points is each color worth?
Which color is worth the most points?
How much did you get when you hit blue twice and red once?

Integrated Curriculum Activities
Allow children to paint by blowing the paint with a straw.
Allow children to move balls in the water table by blowing through a straw or using a baster.

Helpful Hints

Limiting the children to two or three cotton swabs per turn may encourage them to add their scores. Otherwise, they may just keep shooting the swabs. You might prefer to allow unlimited swab shooting in the beginning and later alter the game by limiting the number of swabs and adding a score sheet.

Allow the children to determine how many points each circle on the target is worth.

7.9 Target Ball

Description
Children play this game by throwing balls at a felt target. Velcro on the balls sticks to the target. Score sheets are divided into thirds to match the three colors of the target. Children can keep track of how many balls stick to each color by recording the results on the score sheets or by using beads on an abacus.

Materials
▲ large, circular target made of three colors of felt
▲ 3 to 6 plastic balls with Velcro pieces attached
▲ abacus, or score sheets and pencils, for scorekeeping

Child's Level
This activity appeals to both preschool and kindergarten children. Younger children are interested in the physical-knowledge challenge of hitting the target. Older children focus on quantification and scorekeeping.

What to Look For
Children will experiment with how to throw the balls to get them to adhere to the target.
Children may keep throwing the balls until they all stick to the target.
Children may use an abacus to record their scores.
Children may notate their scores in their own manner on the score sheets.

Helpful Hints

Since there is no point value indicated on the target, children can decide if they want each color to be worth a certain amount.

Use lightweight balls or they will not adhere to the target.

Use self-adhesive Velcro pieces.

Modification
Provide more balls to increase the difficulty of the game.

Questions to Extend Thinking
How many balls are on the target?
Which color has the fewest balls?
How many more balls does red have than yellow?
Is there a way to show how many balls you have on each color?

Integrated Curriculum Activity
Plan a Velcro paddleball game as another gross-motor activity.

7.10 Ski-Ball

Description
Create a ramp that slopes upward to about 12 to 18 inches from the floor at its highest point. A wide slide, two side-by-side wooden planks, slanted hollow blocks, or heavy cardboard are all possibilities. Children play the game by positioning three large cans on the floor at the high end of the ramp, rolling balls up the ramp, and attempting to get the balls into the cans. Score sheets are divided into three sections and are color coded to match the cans.

Materials
- ▲ wide ramp
- ▲ 3 to 6 tennis balls
- ▲ 3 empty 3-pound cans, each covered with a different color of paper
- ▲ score sheets and pencils

Child's Level
This activity is most appropriate for older preschool and kindergarten children. Younger children have difficulty rolling the balls up the ramp, but they enjoy rolling them down the incline.

What to Look For
Children will experiment with where to place the cans and how hard to roll the balls.
Children may try to get all the balls into the cans.
Some children will assign point values to each color of can and attempt to add their scores.

Modification
Use fewer balls for younger children and more balls for older children.

Questions to Extend Thinking
How many balls went into the cans?
How many points do you think each can should be worth?

Integrated Curriculum Activities
Put a marble track in the manipulative area.
Dip marbles into paint and roll them across paper.
Put ramps in the science area with a variety of objects to roll down them.

Helpful Hint

This game requires substantial experimentation. You may choose to delay introducing the score sheets until the children have acquired some mastery of the game.

7.11 Pendulum Bottle Game

Description

A pendulum is constructed by suspending a plastic jar filled with a medium-weight substance such as pasta from a height of about six feet. We hung ours from a tire swing A-frame. The children decide where to place plastic bottles and try to knock them over with the pendulum. They can keep track of how many bottles they knock down if they are interested.

Materials

- ▲ large teacher-made pendulum
- ▲ 6 empty 2-liter plastic bottles
- ▲ paper and pencil

Child's Level

This activity is appropriate for all levels. Young children explore the physical-knowledge aspects of the pendulum and gain information by watching older children knock down the bottles. While older children are also challenged by the physical properties of the pendulum, they also quantify and keep score.

What to Look For

Children will spend a long time experimenting with trying to hit the bottles with the pendulum.

Some children will count to see how many bottles they knocked down.

Some children will record how many bottles they knocked down.

Helpful Hint

Anticipate a lengthy period of experimentation. Children expect the pendulum to respond the same way a ball does when thrown. It does not.

Modifications

Change the weight of the jar by altering the contents. Rocks or cotton balls produce very different results.

Change the weight of the bottles by adding water.

Raise the height of the pendulum by shortening the rope.

Questions to Extend Thinking

Is there another place to put this bottle so that the pendulum will knock it down?

How many bottles are left?

How many bottles fell down?

Why doesn't the pendulum ever hit *this* bottle?

Integrated Curriculum Activities

Add a small pendulum to the science area of the classroom.

Make sand pictures with a pendulum by letting colored sand drip from a jar.

7.12 Pulley Transfer Game

Description
Construct a horizontal pulley between two A-frames or along the back of a shelf, or use a commercial pulley frame. Place a basket of small balls at each end of the pulley. One child stands by each basket. They take turns rolling a giant die and sending a corresponding number of balls to the other person. The game ends when one of the baskets is empty.

Materials
▲ horizontal pulley
▲ 2 baskets with 10 small balls in each
▲ giant die

Child's Level
This self-leveling game is appropriate for all ages. Young children explore the physical properties of the pulley. Older children combine this exploration with quantification.

What to Look For
Some children will use the die to decide how many balls to send.
Some children will disregard the die and just send balls via the pulley.

Pulley and frame pictured here available from
Center Concepts, Incorporated
2414 Ashland Avenue
Cincinnati, Ohio 45206

Modification
Reduce the number of dots on the die to three if six are too many.

Questions to Extend Thinking
How did you decide how many balls to send to Carol?
Which basket has fewer balls now?
How many balls do you have left?
What will happen if you roll a two?

Helpful Hint

If the children seem inclined to use the balls as throwing toys, substitute another item such as cubes or plastic fruit.

Integrated Curriculum Activity
Create a vertical pulley, perhaps to send items up and down a climber.

7.13 Animal Mail-Order Game

Description
Children take turns ordering bears and cats from each other. They place their order by stamping bears and cats onto a card. The child filling the order places a corresponding number of teddy bear and kitty cat counters into the pulley basket and transfers it to the child placing the order.

Materials
- ▲ horizontal pulley
- ▲ 2 bowls of mixed teddy bear and kitty cat counters
- ▲ file cards or slips of paper
- ▲ teddy bear and kitty cat rubber stamps

Child's Level
This game is self leveling but is especially appropriate for older preschool and kindergarten children since it involves creating and comparing sets of two attributes (type of counter and amount). Younger children nevertheless gain valuable physical knowledge by manipulating the pulley. They may disregard the cards but talk about quantities of counters.

Pulley and frame pictured here available from Center Concepts, Incorporated 2414 Ashland Avenue Cincinnati, Ohio 45206

What to Look For
Children may attempt to construct matching sets to fill the orders. Some children will be interested primarily in working the pulley. Children will discuss and debate whether the orders have been filled correctly.

Modification
If quantifying two types of animals is too overwhelming, use either teddy bears or kitty cats.

Questions to Extend Thinking
Did Lydia order more bears or cats?
How did you decide how many bears to put into the basket?

Integrated Curriculum Activities
Create a vertical pulley, perhaps to send items up and down a climber.
Add teddy bear and kitty cat rubber stamps to the writing or art area.

Helpful Hint

You may wish to give the children some experience with the pulley before introducing the rubber stamps.

ANECDOTE 1

Tory (age 5) played a game with beanbags and a target divided into three circles. She decided that the biggest circle would be worth 10, the middle-sized circle 20, and the smallest circle 30. The first child scored 30, 10, and 20. Tory started with 30 and counted 10 more on her fingers to add 10 to 30. Then she thought for a while and continued counting 20 more. She used stable-order counting to 59 and the teacher gave her the word for 60.

Tory took her turn and scored 30 and 30. She started making marks to help her find the total but got tired. Tory then decided that 30 might be the same as 20 and 10. When she counted on from 30 to add the second 30, however, she counted only 10 more and ended up with 40. Although Tory did not get the correct answer, she created a very difficult math problem for herself and devised a strategy to solve it.

ANECDOTE 2

Jonathan (age 4½) enjoyed playing path games in his classroom. He usually correctly counted the number of dots on two dice and then moved the same number of spaces along the path; however, he always re-counted the space his mover occupied when he began a new turn.

Jonathan was excited when he saw a path game in the gross-motor room. He quickly joined in the play. Jonathan rolled the giant die and hopped a corresponding number of spaces along the path. When it was time for his next turn, he did not re-count the space he already occupied; instead, he moved forward for his first hop.

After two weeks of hopping along the path in the gross-motor room, Jonathan no longer re-counted the space his mover was on when playing board games in the classroom.

ANECDOTE 3

Charlie (age 4) was interested in the large pendulum that had been attached to the tire-swing frame in the outside play area. He set up the bottles in a row and swung the pendulum. It sailed over the top of the bottles without touching them. Charlie tried again with the same result. When he observed that the pendulum did not reach the bottles, he threw it as hard as he could. Again it went over the top of the bottles without hitting them. Other children joined Charlie and also tried to knock the bottles over without success. Charlie said, "I guess it's broken."

After two days of unsuccessfully trying to hit the bottles, Charlie decided to put the bottles in the center of the pendulum frame. This time, when he swung the pendulum, it knocked the bottles down.

Later, another child lined up the bottles along the edge of the pendulum frame and tried to knock them down with the pendulum. The pendulum swung over the top of the bottles. Charlie ran over. "You have to put the bottles here," he said, pointing to the center of the pendulum frame.

CHAPTER 8

The Math Suitcase

"Oh boy! Oh, boy! It's my turn for the math suitcase!" Tony's excitement at finding the math suitcase in his cubby is typical of many preschoolers since its introduction into our program.

Teachers are constantly looking for ways to connect home and school. After having success with sending writing suitcases home, we began looking for a means to also share our math curriculum with parents. We wanted to show parents alternatives to workbooks. The result was our math suitcase.

Teachers' Questions

What is a math suitcase?

The math suitcase is a take-home kit that contains math games similar to those used in the classroom. It is modeled after the writing suitcase introduced by Susan Rich (see "The Writing Suitcase" in *Young Children*, July 1985). Children take turns bringing math games home in a small plastic carrying case and playing them with their families. The goals for the math suitcase are to increase children's opportunities to construct logical-mathematical relationships, to educate parents about appropriate ways to facilitate this development, and especially to encourage parents and children to enjoy math experiences together.

Why is the math suitcase an important part of the math curriculum?

The math suitcase is a bridge between home and school. Parents are important educators of their children. The math suitcase is fun and nonthreatening. It educates parents about how children construct mathematical knowledge so that they can become facilitators of this process.

Children love the math suitcase! Although they are actually processing higher-level math concepts than many of them will have when they begin traditional school, they think it's fun. Typical children's comments are—

- ▲ I love the math suitcase.
- ▲ Math is fun.
- ▲ I'm good at math.

In writing to thank his child's teacher for sending home the math suitcase, a father listed these additional benefits (we thank Anthony Tsai for his letter):

▲ The child feels special.

▲ The child learns accountability/stewardship.

▲ The parents co-work with the child.

▲ Skill development increases.

▲ Task completion is encouraged.

▲ Teacher/parent interaction is encouraged.

What goes into the math suitcase?

The math suitcase contains—

▲ one or more games,

▲ a letter to parents, and

▲ a reminder letter that tells the child when to bring it back.

The types of games and dice used in the math suitcase are varied according to the level of the individual child. Smaller versions of grid games and path games are often used. The dice, counters, and movers are contained in a Ziploc bag. Card games and commercial travel games are sometimes included for older children.

The teacher-constructed games are made with stickers and poster board and are laminated. The counters are usually either marble chips or designer erasers, since these are inexpensive to replace and a few pieces are sometimes lost.

The parent letter briefly explains how children construct mathematical concepts. It cautions parents not to correct errors, but gives them examples of questions they can use to facilitate mathematical thinking. It also warns parents to keep the suitcase away from younger siblings since it contains small pieces.

The child's letter is printed to reinforce emerging literacy. It tells the child when to bring the suitcase back and might look like the example below.

Dear Jessica,
Have fun with the math suitcase.
Please bring it back on Tuesday.
Brenda

How do children and parents know how to play the games?

The math suitcase games are smaller versions of classroom math games that the children are familiar with. They play them in the same ways. The letter to the parents encourages them to ask children how to play the games and to allow children to devise new rules if they wish, since this helps children play the games at a level appropriate for them.

How often should the math suitcase be sent home?

Several times a year.

Our classrooms each have sixteen children. Some teachers send home four suitcases per week, so that each child gets a turn about once a month. Other teachers send home two suitcases per week, so the children get a turn every other month. The suitcases are usually sent home first with children in their second year of preschool, since they are already familiar with playing math games.

Some teachers send the math suitcase home on Thursday and have the children return it on Tuesday. This gives the teacher two days to refurbish it. A math suitcase schedule is posted on the class bulletin board since the children are eager to know when it will be their turn to take it home.

How should teachers decide what to put into the math suitcase for each child?

Teachers should check their anecdotal notes or assessment sheets and plan accordingly. If a child is not yet able to play path games, then perhaps just a grid game should be included. A 1-3 or 1-6 die should be selected depending on the child's level of quantification.

If a child is using path games in the classroom, then both a grid game and a path game could be included. If the child is combining two dice by counting the dots (whether or not errors are made), then two dice should be included.

For children who are very secure with teacher-made path games, commercial, travel-size path games can be considered. The smaller path may be more exciting and challenging.

Card games such as "war" are more difficult than grid and path games. They are generally reserved for older or more advanced children.

What has been the response to the math suitcase?

Overwhelmingly positive! Children dance up and down when they see the suitcase in their cubbies. Parents seem equally excited and often send back thank you notes. This note from a four-year-old child seems to express the enthusiasm felt by many.

Math Suitcase Activities

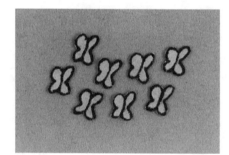

The following math suitcases are arranged in order of difficulty with suitcase 8.1 being the easiest.

8.1 Cloud Math Suitcase

Materials
Cloud grid game
- ▲ 2 game boards, 8 by 5¾ inches, made from blue poster board, each with 12 cloud stickers
- ▲ 24 rainbow erasers or 24 clear marble chips that look like raindrops for counters
- ▲ 1-3 die made from a blue 1-inch cube and silver raindrop stickers

9 by 6-inch case

Child's Level
This is the easiest math suitcase. It is most appropriate for children working on one-to-one correspondence or quantification to three.

8.2 Flower Basket Math Suitcase

Materials

Flower basket grid game

▲ 2 game boards, 8 by 6 inches, made from green poster board, each with 15 flower basket stickers

▲ 30 flower chips for counters

▲ 1-3 die

Flower basket short path game

▲ 2 game boards, 17 by 5 inches, made from green poster board, each with round stickers leading to a flower basket sticker

▲ 2 watering can movers

▲ 1-3 die

13 by 9-inch case

Child's Level

This suitcase is for children who are beginning to move an equivalent number of spaces along a path. The path is short, straight, and simple. The grid game reinforces concepts of one-to-one correspondence and creation of equivalent sets. A 1-6 die can be used for children quantifying beyond three.

8.3 Snowman Math Suitcase

Materials

Snowman grid game
- ▲ 2 game boards, 6 by 12 inches, made from black poster board, each with 12 snowman stickers
- ▲ 24 snowman erasers for counters
- ▲ 1-6 die

Snowman path game
- ▲ 1 or 2 game boards, 15 by 5 inches, made from red poster board with 16 round stickers leading to a snowman sticker
- ▲ 2 wooden people movers
- ▲ 1-6 die

13 by 9-inch case

Child's Level

This suitcase is designed for children who are comfortable with a slightly more complex path and quantification to six.

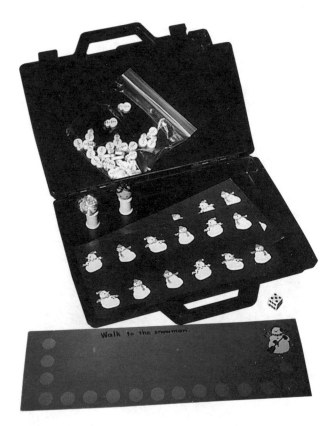

8.4 Dinosaur Math Suitcase

Materials

Fossil grid game

- ▲ 2 game boards, 8 by 5¾ inches, made from white poster board, each with 12 small bones cut from black construction paper
- ▲ 24 small fossils or pebbles for counters
- ▲ 1-6 die

Dinosaur path game

- ▲ 1 game board made from white poster board, 17 by 5 inches, with 24 small black bone cutouts leading from a fossil hunter to a museum
- ▲ 2 small people movers
- ▲ 1 or 2 standard 1-6 dice

9 by 6-inch case

Child's Level

This suitcase is for children able to play a long path game in the classroom. Include two dice for children who are beginning to add (counting all the dots on two dice).

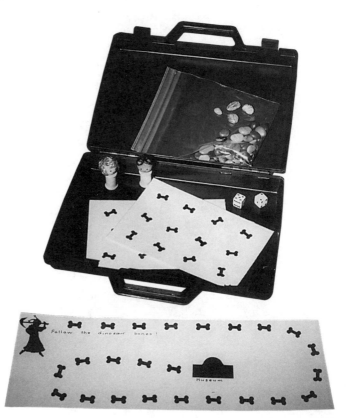

8.5 Butterfly Math Suitcase

Materials

Butterfly chase path game
- ▲ 1 game board, 17 by 5 inches, made from white poster board with 46 tiny butterfly stickers leading from a silhouette sticker to a basket of flowers
- ▲ 2 small people movers
- ▲ 2 standard 1-6 dice

Card game
- ▲ white index cards with ¾-inch circle stickers to show the quantities 1 through 6. Make 4 cards for each number.

9 by 6-inch case

Description

Children can play the card game by dividing the cards and each turning over one card at a time. The person with the higher card value takes both cards. Children can decide what to do if they both turn over the same number. They can also use the cards to play "Memory" or "Go Fish"-type games.

Child's Level

This suitcase is most appropriate for kindergarten. The path game has a longer, more complex path than the game in the dinosaur suitcase (8.4). It is for children who are secure with path games and two dice.

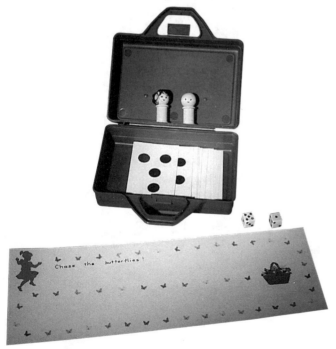

8.6 "Party On" Math Suitcase

Materials

Musical notes grid game

▲ 2 game boards, 8 by 5 ¾ inches, made from white poster board and musical note stickers. The boards are divided into 6 sections with 1 to 6 notes per section

▲ 22 small guitar erasers for counters

▲ 1-6 dice

"Party On" path game

▲ 1 game board, 17 by 5 inches, made from white poster board with 41 musical note stickers leading from 2 children to a party

▲ 2 people movers

▲ 2 1-6 dice

Musical notes card game

▲ White index cards with 1 to 6 musical note stickers per card. Make four cards for each number.

9 by 6-inch case

Description

Children can play the card game by dividing the cards and each turning over one card at a time. The person with the higher card value takes both cards. Children can decide what to do if they both turn over the same number. They can also use the cards to play "Memory" or "Go Fish"-type games.

Child's Level

This suitcase is appropriate for kindergarten. These games are for children who are comfortable playing path games and quantifying with two dice. All three games are a little tricky, since some of the musical notes are beamed (connected). Children must decide whether beamed notes count as one or two.

Interactions with The Math Suitcase

ANECDOTE 1

When Krista (age 4) entered school she showed no concept of quantification. She would point to one object and say "six." She could not take the same number of objects as she rolled on a 1-3 die, and she did not have stable-order counting.

Krista was nonetheless delighted when it was her turn to take the math suitcase home. It contained a simple grid and counter game and a 1-3 die. After having the suitcase for a week, Krista began to correctly quantify small numbers of items on her own initiative. When making a picture, she correctly identified three pumpkins and one scarecrow on her paper. In just one week she had begun to stable-order count and had realized that the last number counted was the total. Krista could now apply this knowledge to new math situations in her life.

ANECDOTE 2

Dena (age 4½) could not wait to take the math suitcase home and play it with her older sister. The teacher noticed that shortly after Dena had had her turn with the math suitcase, she began to add two dice together by counting all the dots. Previously, she had counted the dots on one die and moved that many spaces along the path, and then counted the dots on the second die and moved again. The teacher commented on this to Dena's mother. "Oh yes," said Dena's mother. "She watched her sister Elsie count the dots on both dice together for a few days, and then she suddenly started to do that, too."

ANECDOTE 3

Bonnie (age 5) took home a math suitcase that contained a grid game with heart stickers and red jewel counters, and a path game. The path consisted of alternating gold and silver hearts, and the game had two teddy bear movers and two dice. Bonnie's mother played the games with her and reported to the teacher some interesting modifications that Bonnie made to the rules of the games in order to increase their difficulty.

Bonnie began by playing the games in a typical fashion. She played the grid game by rolling one die and taking an equivalent number of jewels until she had placed one jewel on each heart on her board. Next she played the path game. She rolled both dice, added them together by counting all the dots, and moved her teddy bear an equivalent number of spaces until she reached the end. The game was soon over.

Now Bonnie began to alter the rules and combine the two games. She played the path game again with her mother, but each time they landed on a silver heart they collected a jewel. At the end of the game they counted and compared their jewels.

Bonnie wanted to be able to collect more jewels, so she again revised the rules. This time a player collected a jewel each time she took a turn. Bonnie also got paper and pencil and recorded each player's turn with the appropriate numeral. Because there were so many steps involved in each turn, she and her mother would sometimes lose track of whose turn it was. Bonnie would then count each player's jewels, and whoever had the smallest amount would take the next turn.

At the end of the game, Bonnie looked at the numbers she had written and announced that she had taken ten turns. She counted her jewels and found she had ten, as written. Bonnie then told her mother that she had taken only eight turns. Her mother counted her jewels and verified that she had eight.

Bonnie's mother then asked Bonnie how many more turns she had taken than her mother. Bonnie said ten. Rather than correcting Bonnie, her mother then began to line up her jewels in a row. Bonnie responded by lining her jewels up next to her mother's in one-to-one correspondence.

```
o  o  o  o  o  o  o  o            mother's row
o  o  o  o  o  o  o  o  o  o       Bonnie's row
```

Although Bonnie still didn't answer her mother's question, she moved one jewel from her row to her mother's row and said, There Mom, now we both have ten. Bonnie's mother counted her jewels, and Bonnie also counted hers. They each had nine. Bonnie then took her jewel back and said, Now I have ten and you have eight. This ended the game.

The willingness of Bonnie's mother to allow Bonnie to alter the game rules enabled Bonnie to make the game more challenging. Also, her mother's insightful questions and restraint in correcting Bonnie's errors encouraged Bonnie to think more deeply about a challenging mathematical problem. *Thanks to Cathy Hudson for her letter documenting this interaction.*

Appendix

A.1 Class Assessment Form

Material:

child	outcome		strategy			errors			addition			comments
	free play	makes sets	global	1:1	counts	stable-order to	skips	re-counts	counts all	adds on	knows comb.	

More Than Counting

A.2 Individual Assessment Form

Child:

date	material	outcome		strategy		errors			addition			comments
		free play	makes sets	global	1:1	counts	stable-order to	skips	re-counts	counts all	adds on	knows comb.	

A.3 Class Assessment Form for Collections

Collection: Date:

Name	Sorts by					

A.4 Individual Assessment Form for Collections

Child:

Collection	Sorts by, Date					

Three Little Bats
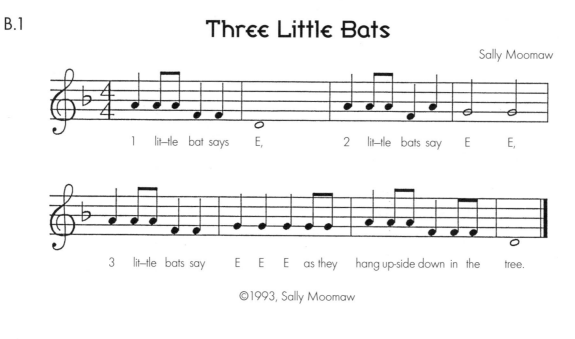

B.1

Sally Moomaw

1 lit—tle bat says E,   2 lit—tle bats say E E,

3 lit—tle bats say E E E as they hang up-side down in the tree.

©1993, Sally Moomaw

Salty Pretzels

B.2

Brenda Hieronymus

1 sal—ty pret — zel, 2 sal—ty pret — zels, 3 sal—ty pret — zels,

4, We'll roll and roll and shape and bake and then make ma — ny more.

©1986, Brenda Hieronymus

B.3

It Was Snow

Sally Moomaw

It looked like balls of cot—ton, It looked like cook—ie dough,

It looked like my white blan—ket, It was snow, snow, snow.

©1978, 1980, Sally Moomaw

Glossary

addends	Quantities that contribute to a sum; for example, in the statement $3 + 1 = 4$, 3 and 1 are the addends that result in the sum, 4.
add on	To add two sets by recognizing the quantity of the first set and then counting on without re-counting the first set.
assessment form	A tool for recording the developmental progress of an individual child or a whole class in general.
attribute	A characteristic of an object; for example, color, shape, or size.
autonomous	Independent; adamant about asserting one's self and making one's own decisions.
cardinality	The stage of quantification where the child realizes that the last number counted represents the total.
classification of materials	The grouping of objects by a particular attribute.
cognitive	Referring to intellectual development.
collection	A group of objects for children to sort and classify by various attributes.
collection game	A path game where collection pieces are added.
comparison of sets	A consideration of the relationship between sets in order to determine their similarities or differences in quantities.
construct math concepts	To develop, or more accurately, to invent, logical-mathematical knowledge through relationships that are formed as children interact with objects and think about the results.
constructivist	One who prescribes to Piagetian theory (named for Jean Piaget) that children construct, or develop, knowledge through their actions on the environment.
continuous path game	A long path game that does not have a definite start and finish point; usually shaped in a square, oval, or circle.
developmentally appropriate	Pertaining to materials and classroom environments that are matched to the developmental characteristics of groups of young children as well as individual children.
division of materials	A system for separating materials into groups judged by the child to be equal.
double-counting	When quantifying, to count some objects more than once.
equivalent sets	Two sets that contain the same quantity of objects.
free play	Imaginative play, not necessarily involving math.
global stage	The stage of quantification where the child quantifies perceptually.
graphs, class	Bar graphs that are carefully designed to help children record class voting responses.
grid game	Math game played on cards with spaces on which to put counters in a one-to-one correspondence relationship.